best of the best
ONE DISH

Publications International, Ltd.
Favorite Brand Name Recipes at www.fbnr.com

Microwave Cooking: Microwave ovens vary in wattage. Use the cooking times as guidelines and check for doneness before adding more time.

Preparation/Cooking Times: Preparation times are based on the approximate amount of time required to assemble the recipe before cooking, baking, chilling or serving. These times include preparation steps such as measuring, chopping and mixing. The fact that some preparations and cooking can be done simultaneously is taken into account. Preparation of optional ingredients and serving suggestions is not included.

contents

✳ ✳ ✳

homestyle
breakfast & brunch

Delicious Ham & Cheese Puff Pie

2 cups (about 1 pound) diced cooked ham

1 package (10 ounces) frozen chopped spinach, thawed and squeezed dry

½ cup diced red bell pepper

4 green onions, sliced

3 eggs

¾ cup all-purpose flour

¾ cup (3 ounces) shredded Swiss cheese

¾ cup milk

1 tablespoon prepared mustard

1 teaspoon grated lemon peel

1 teaspoon dried dill weed

½ teaspoon garlic salt

½ teaspoon black pepper

Fresh dill sprigs and lemon slices (optional)

1. Preheat oven to 425°F. Grease round 2-quart casserole.

2. Combine ham, spinach, bell pepper and green onions in prepared casserole. Beat eggs in medium bowl. Stir in flour, cheese, milk, mustard, lemon peel, dill weed, garlic salt and black pepper; pour over ham mixture.

3. Bake 30 to 35 minutes or until puffed and browned. Cut into wedges and garnish with fresh dill and lemon slices.

Makes 4 to 6 servings

Aunt Marilyn's Cinnamon French Toast Casserole

    1 large loaf French bread, cut into 1½-inch slices
3½ cups milk
    9 eggs
1½ cups sugar, divided
    1 tablespoon vanilla
    ½ teaspoon salt
    6 to 8 medium baking apples, such as McIntosh or Cortland, peeled
        and sliced
    1 teaspoon ground cinnamon
    ½ teaspoon ground nutmeg
        Powdered sugar

1. Place bread slices in greased 13×9-inch glass baking dish or casserole.

2. Whisk milk, eggs, 1 cup sugar, vanilla and salt in large bowl until well blended. Pour half of mixture over bread.

3. Layer apple slices over bread. Pour remaining egg mixture over apples.

4. Combine remaining ½ cup sugar, cinnamon and nutmeg in small bowl; sprinkle over casserole. Cover and refrigerate overnight.

5. Preheat oven to 350°F. Bake, uncovered, 1 hour or until eggs are set. Sprinkle with powdered sugar. *Makes 6 to 8 servings*

Sausage Scramble

    1 pound BOB EVANS® Original Recipe Roll Sausage
10 ounces (2 cups) BOB EVANS® Diced Seasoned Home Fries
    ⅓ cup chopped green pepper
    8 eggs
    ½ cup milk

In a large skillet over medium heat, crumble and cook sausage, potatoes and green peppers until sausage and potatoes are brown. In a small bowl, combine eggs and milk until mixed well. Pour over sausage and potato mixture, stirring gently until eggs are cooked. Serve warm. *Makes 6 servings*

Aunt Marilyn's Cinnamon French
Toast Casserole

Chile-Corn Quiche

1 (9-inch) pastry shell, 1½ inches deep
1 can (about 8 ounces) corn, drained *or* 1 cup frozen corn, cooked
1 can (4 ounces) diced mild green chiles, drained
¼ cup thinly sliced green onions
1 cup (4 ounces) shredded Monterey Jack cheese
3 eggs
1½ cups half-and-half
½ teaspoon salt
½ teaspoon ground cumin

1. Preheat oven to 450°F. Line pastry shell with foil; partially fill with pie weights or dried beans to weight shell. Bake 10 minutes. Remove foil and weights; continue baking pastry 5 minutes or until lightly browned. Set aside to cool. *Reduce oven temperature to 375°F.*

2. Combine corn, green chiles and green onions in small bowl. Spoon into pastry shell; sprinkle with cheese. Whisk eggs, half-and-half, salt and cumin in medium bowl; pour over cheese.

3. Bake 35 to 45 minutes or until filling is puffed and knife inserted in center comes out clean. Let stand 10 minutes before serving.

Makes 6 servings

note

Using pie weights or dried beans will help to keep the shape of the pie crust. This will ensure that the filling stays inside the pie during baking. Look for pie weights at any cookware or baking specialty store.

Chili-Corn Quiche

Spicy Crabmeat Frittata

1 can (6½ ounces) lump white crabmeat, drained
1 tablespoon olive oil
1 medium green bell pepper, finely chopped
2 cloves garlic, minced
6 eggs
¼ teaspoon salt
¼ teaspoon black pepper
¼ teaspoon hot pepper sauce
1 large plum tomato, seeded and finely chopped

1. Break up large pieces of crabmeat, picking out and discarding any shell or cartilage. Preheat broiler. Heat oil in 10-inch nonstick skillet with ovenproof handle over medium-high heat. Add bell pepper and garlic; cook and stir 3 minutes or until soft.

2. Meanwhile, beat eggs in medium bowl. Add crabmeat, salt, black pepper and hot pepper sauce to eggs; blend well. Set aside.

3. Add tomato to skillet; cook and stir 1 minute. Add egg mixture. Reduce heat to medium-low; cook about 7 minutes or until eggs begin to set around edges.

4. Place skillet under broiler 6 inches from heat. Broil about 2 minutes or until frittata is set and top is browned. Remove from broiler; slide frittata onto serving plate. Serve immediately.

Makes 4 servings

Serving Suggestion: Serve with crusty bread, cut-up raw vegetables and guacamole.

Prep and Cook Time: 20 minutes

Spicy Crabmeat Frittata

Ham 'n' Apple Breakfast Casserole

1 package (15 ounces) refrigerated pie crusts (2 crusts)
1 pound thinly sliced ham, cut into bite-size pieces
1 can (21 ounces) apple pie filling
1 cup (4 ounces) shredded sharp Cheddar cheese
¼ cup plus 1 teaspoon sugar, divided
½ teaspoon ground cinnamon

1. Preheat oven to 425°F.

2. Place one crust in 9-inch pie pan, allowing edges to hang over sides. Arrange half of ham pieces on bottom crust. Spoon apple filling onto ham. Top with remaining ham; sprinkle with cheese.

3. Mix ¼ cup sugar and cinnamon in small bowl; sprinkle evenly over cheese. Place second crust over filling; crimp edges together. Brush crust lightly with water; sprinkle with remaining 1 teaspoon sugar. Cut slits for steam to escape.

4. Bake 20 to 25 minutes or until crust is golden brown. Cool 15 minutes. Slice into wedges. *Makes 6 servings*

Tip: This casserole can be assembled the night before, covered, refrigerated and baked the next morning.

Ham 'n' Apple Breakfast Casserole

Tortilla Frittata

8 eggs
1 cup ORTEGA® Salsa, any variety
½ teaspoon salt
½ teaspoon black pepper
4 ORTEGA® Yellow Corn Taco Shells, crushed
1 cup chopped mushrooms
½ cup chopped tomato
½ cup chopped green onions
1½ cups shredded taco cheese blend

In large bowl, whisk together eggs, salsa, salt and pepper. Crumble yellow corn taco shells over egg mixture and soak 10 minutes.

Preheat oven to 400°F.

Cook and stir mushrooms, tomato and green onions 4 minutes in well-oiled ovenproof skillet over medium-high heat. Spread ingredients evenly around pan. Pour in egg mixture and spread out evenly in pan. Cook about 2 minutes or until eggs begin to cook around sides.

Remove skillet from heat and sprinkle cheese over top. Place in oven and bake 10 minutes or until frittata begins to puff up and brown.

Serve frittata right out of skillet or transfer to serving plate and cut into pieces. *Makes 6 to 8 servings*

Note: For a great presentation, bring the frittata to the table garnished with cilantro, sour cream and guacamole.

Prep Time: 20 minutes
Start to Finish: 40 minutes

Tortilla Frittata

Steak Hash

2 tablespoons vegetable oil
1 green bell pepper, chopped
½ medium onion, chopped
1 pound russet potatoes, baked and chopped
½ pound cooked steak or roast beef, cut into 1-inch cubes
    Salt and black pepper
½ cup (2 ounces) shredded Monterey Jack cheese
4 poached or fried eggs

1. Heat oil in large skillet over medium heat. Add bell pepper and onion; cook until tender. Stir in potatoes; reduce heat to low. Cover and cook about 10 minutes or until potatoes are heated through, stirring occasionally.

2. Stir in steak; season with salt and black pepper. Sprinkle with cheese. Cover; cook 5 minutes or until steak is heated through and cheese is melted.

3. Top each serving of hash with 1 egg.   *Makes 4 servings*

Brunch Casserole

1 pound mild bulk pork sausage
3 cups frozen hash brown potatoes, thawed
1 cup diced green bell pepper
1 can (11 ounces) condensed nacho cheese soup, undiluted
¼ cup milk
1 cup (4 ounces) shredded Cheddar cheese

1. Preheat oven to 350°F. Coat 11×7-inch casserole with nonstick cooking spray.

2. Brown sausage in large skillet over medium-high heat, stirring to break up meat. Drain fat. Combine potatoes, bell pepper and two thirds of soup in medium bowl. Spoon into prepared casserole. Layer sausage over potato mixture. Stir together remaining one third of soup and milk in small bowl. Pour over sausage. Sprinkle with cheese.

3. Bake 20 minutes or until cheese is melted and sauce is slightly bubbly.   *Makes 4 to 6 servings*

Steak Hash

Ham and Egg Enchiladas

  2 tablespoons butter
  1 small red bell pepper, chopped
  3 green onions, sliced
  ½ cup diced ham
  8 eggs
  8 (7- to 8-inch) flour tortillas
  ½ cup (2 ounces) shredded pepper jack cheese
  1 can (10 ounces) enchilada sauce
  ½ cup salsa
  1½ cups (6 ounces) shredded pepper jack cheese (optional)

1. Preheat oven to 350°F.

2. Melt butter in large nonstick skillet over medium heat. Add bell pepper and onions; cook and stir 2 minutes. Add ham; cook and stir 1 minute.

3. Lightly beat eggs in medium bowl. Add eggs to skillet; cook until eggs are set but still soft, stirring occasionally.

4. Spoon about ⅓ cup egg mixture evenly down center of each tortilla; top with 1 tablespoon cheese. Roll up tortillas and place seam side down in shallow 11×7-inch baking dish.

5. Combine enchilada sauce and salsa in small bowl; pour evenly over enchiladas.

6. Cover dish with foil; bake 20 minutes. Uncover; sprinkle with 1½ cups cheese, if desired. Continue baking 10 minutes or until enchiladas are heated through and cheese is melted. Serve immediately. *Makes 4 servings*

Cheese Grits with Chiles and Bacon

6 strips bacon
1 serrano or jalapeño pepper,* cored, seeded and minced
1 large shallot or small onion, finely chopped
4 cups chicken broth
1 cup grits**
½ teaspoon salt
¼ teaspoon black pepper
½ cup half-and-half
1 cup (4 ounces) shredded Cheddar cheese
2 tablespoons finely chopped green onion, green part only

*Hot peppers can sting and irritate the skin, so wear rubber gloves when handling peppers and do not touch eyes.

**You may use coarse, instant, yellow or stone-ground grits.

Slow Cooker Directions

1. Fry bacon on both sides in medium skillet until crisp. Remove bacon and drain on paper towels. Drain all but 1 tablespoon bacon drippings from skillet. Crumble 2 strips of bacon; place in slow cooker. Reserve remaining bacon.

2. Add serrano pepper and shallot to skillet. Cook and stir over medium-high heat 1 minute or until shallot is transparent and lightly browned. Transfer to slow cooker. Stir in broth, grits, salt and black pepper. Cover; cook on LOW 4 hours.

3. Stir in half-and-half and cheese. Sprinkle with green onion. Crumble remaining bacon into bite-size pieces; stir into grits or sprinkle on top of each serving. Serve immediately.

Makes 4 servings

Prep Time: 15 minutes
Cook Time: 4 hours

Blueberry-Orange French Toast Casserole

6 slices whole wheat bread, cut into 1-inch pieces
1 cup fresh blueberries
½ cup sugar
½ cup milk
2 eggs
4 egg whites
1 tablespoon grated orange peel
½ teaspoon vanilla

1. Preheat oven to 350°F. Coat 8-inch square baking dish with nonstick cooking spray. Place bread and blueberries in dish; toss gently to combine.

2. Whisk sugar into milk in medium bowl until dissolved. Whisk in eggs, egg whites, orange peel and vanilla; pour over bread mixture. Toss to coat. Let stand 5 minutes.

3. Bake 40 to 45 minutes or until top of bread is browned and center is almost set. Let stand 5 minutes.   *Makes 6 servings*

Spicy Sausage Skillet Breakfast

2 bags SUCCESS® Rice
Nonstick cooking spray
1 pound bulk turkey sausage
½ cup chopped onion
1 can (10 ounces) tomatoes with green chilies, undrained
1 tablespoon chili powder
1 cup (4 ounces) shredded reduced-fat Monterey Jack cheese

Prepare rice according to package directions.

Lightly coat large skillet with cooking spray. Crumble sausage into prepared skillet. Cook over medium heat until lightly browned, stirring occasionally. Add onion; cook until tender. Stir in tomatoes, chili powder and rice; simmer 2 minutes. Reduce heat to low. Simmer until no liquid remains, about 8 minutes, stirring occasionally. Sprinkle with cheese.   *Makes 6 servings*

Blueberry-Orange French Toast Casserole

Spinach Sensation

½ **pound sliced bacon**

1 **cup (8 ounces) sour cream**

3 **eggs, separated**

2 **tablespoons all-purpose flour**

⅛ **teaspoon black pepper**

1 **package (10 ounces) frozen chopped spinach, thawed and squeezed dry**

½ **cup (2 ounces) shredded sharp Cheddar cheese**

½ **cup dry bread crumbs**

1 **tablespoon butter, melted**

1. Preheat oven to 350°F. Spray 2-quart round baking dish with nonstick cooking spray.

2. Place bacon in single layer in large skillet; cook over medium heat until crisp. Remove from skillet; drain on paper towels. Crumble and set aside.

3. Combine sour cream, egg yolks, flour and pepper in large bowl; set aside. Beat egg whites in medium bowl with electric mixer at high speed until stiff peaks form. Stir one fourth of egg whites into sour cream mixture; fold in remaining egg whites.

4. Arrange half of spinach in prepared dish. Top with half of sour cream mixture. Sprinkle with ¼ cup cheese. Sprinkle bacon over cheese. Repeat layers, ending with cheese.

5. Combine bread crumbs and butter in small bowl; sprinkle evenly over cheese. Bake, uncovered, 30 to 35 minutes or until egg mixture is set. Let stand 5 minutes before serving.   *Makes 6 servings*

Spinach Sensation

Breakfast Bake

1 pound ground pork sausage

1 teaspoon Italian seasoning

½ teaspoon salt

6 eggs

2 cups milk

½ cup CREAM OF WHEAT® Hot Cereal (Instant, 1-minute, 2½-minute or 10-minute cook time), uncooked

1 teaspoon TRAPPEY'S® Red Devil™ Cayenne Pepper Sauce

4 cups cubed bread stuffing (potato bread recommended)

2 cups Cheddar cheese, shredded

1. Brown sausage in skillet, pressing with fork or spatula to crumble as it cooks. Sprinkle on Italian seasoning and salt; set aside.

2. Combine eggs, milk, Cream of Wheat and pepper sauce in large mixing bowl; mix well. Add cooked sausage and bread stuffing; toss to combine. Pour mixture into 13×9-inch casserole pan; cover. Refrigerate at least 4 hours or overnight.

3. Preheat oven to 350°F. Remove cover and sprinkle cheese over casserole. Cover pan with aluminum foil; bake 30 minutes. Remove foil; bake 15 minutes longer. Serve warm.   *Makes 8 servings*

Prep Time: 30 minutes
Start to Finish Time: 4 to 12 hours soaking, 45 minutes baking

Corned Beef Hash

2 large russet potatoes, peeled and cut into ½-inch cubes

½ teaspoon salt

¼ teaspoon black pepper

¼ cup (½ stick) butter

1 large onion, chopped

½ pound corned beef, finely chopped

1 tablespoon prepared horseradish

¼ cup whipping cream (optional)

4 poached or fried eggs

continued on page 26

Breakfast Bake

Corned Beef Hash, continued

1. Place potatoes in 10-inch skillet; cover with water. Bring to a boil over high heat. Reduce heat to low; simmer 6 minutes. (Potatoes will be firm.) Drain potatoes; remove to plate. Sprinkle with salt and pepper.

2. Wipe out skillet with paper towel. Add butter and onion; cook and stir over medium-high heat 5 minutes. Stir in corned beef, horseradish and potatoes; mix well. Press down with spatula to flatten into compact layer.

3. Reduce heat to low. Drizzle cream evenly over mixture, if desired. Cook 10 to 15 minutes. Flip with spatula; pat down and continue cooking 10 to 15 minutes or until bottom is well browned. Top each serving with 1 poached egg. Serve immediately.

Makes 4 servings

Biscuit and Sausage Bake

2 cups biscuit baking mix
½ cup milk
1 egg
1 teaspoon vanilla
1 cup fresh or frozen blueberries
6 fully cooked breakfast sausage links, thawed if frozen
Maple syrup, warmed

1. Preheat oven to 350°F. Spray 8-inch square baking pan with nonstick cooking spray.

2. Whisk baking mix, milk, egg and vanilla in medium bowl. Fold in blueberries. (Batter will be stiff.) Spread batter in prepared pan.

3. Cut each sausage link into small pieces; sprinkle over batter.

4. Bake 22 minutes or until lightly browned on top. Cut into squares; serve with maple syrup.

Makes 6 servings

Prep Time: 10 minutes
Bake Time: 22 minutes

Biscuit and Sausage Bake

Spanish Omelet with Red Potatoes

4 small red potatoes, quartered
2 tablespoons olive oil
½ cup onion, diced
½ cup green bell pepper, diced
½ cup red bell pepper, diced
2 tablespoons ORTEGA® Diced Green Chiles
½ pound Italian turkey sausage, sliced
8 eggs
½ cup ORTEGA® Salsa, any variety
1 teaspoon dried oregano
   Nonstick cooking spray
½ cup shredded Cheddar cheese
   Additional ORTEGA® Salsa, any variety (optional)

Bring water to a boil in small saucepan. Add potatoes and cook 8 minutes or until softened. Drain and set aside.

Heat oil in skillet over medium heat. Add onion, peppers, diced green chiles and sausage. Cook vegetables and meat about 5 minutes, stirring often, until meat is cooked through.

In separate bowl, whisk together eggs, salsa and oregano.

Spray small skillet or omelet pan with nonstick cooking spray. For each omelet, pour in one-fourth egg mixture and begin heating. Add one-fourth pepper mixture and one-fourth potatoes. With spatula, pull back eggs from sides to allow uncooked eggs to cook through. Cook omelet until it begins to harden, about 4 minutes. Flip omelet over and cook an additional 4 minutes. Sprinkle with cheese and additional salsa, if desired.

Makes 4 large servings or 8 small servings

Prep Time: 15 minutes
Start to Finish: 30 minutes

Spanish Omelet with Red Potatoes

Chile Cheese Puff

¾ **cup all-purpose flour**
1½ **teaspoons baking powder**
9 **eggs**
4 **cups (16 ounces) shredded Monterey Jack cheese**
2 **cups (16 ounces) cottage cheese**
2 **cans (4 ounces each) diced green chiles, drained**
1½ **teaspoons sugar**
¼ **teaspoon salt**
⅛ **teaspoon hot pepper sauce**
1 **cup salsa**

1. Preheat oven to 350°F. Spray 13×9-inch baking dish with nonstick cooking spray.

2. Combine flour and baking powder in small bowl.

3. Whisk eggs in large bowl until blended; stir in Monterey Jack cheese, cottage cheese, chiles, sugar, salt and hot pepper sauce. Add flour mixture; stir just until blended. Pour into prepared dish.

4. Bake, uncovered, 45 minutes or until set. Let stand 5 minutes before serving. Serve with salsa.   *Makes 8 servings*

note

Breakfast casseroles are always a hit. You can customize this easy dish by adding diced cooked chicken, thawed frozen corn or sautéed onions.

Chile Cheese Puff

Chocolate-Stuffed Slow Cooker French Toast

6 slices (¾ inch thick) day-old challah bread*
½ cup semisweet chocolate chips, divided
6 eggs
2 cups half-and-half
1 cup milk
⅔ cup sugar
1 teaspoon vanilla
¼ teaspoon salt
   Powdered sugar or warm maple syrup
   Fresh fruit (optional)

Challah is usually braided. If you use brioche or another rich egg bread, slice bread to fit baking dish.

Slow Cooker Directions

1. Generously grease 2½-quart baking dish that fits inside 6-quart slow cooker. Arrange 2 bread slices in bottom of dish. Sprinkle with ¼ cup chocolate chips. Top with 2 more bread slices. Sprinkle with remaining ¼ cup chocolate chips. Top with remaining 2 bread slices.

2. Beat eggs in large bowl. Stir in half-and-half, milk, sugar, vanilla and salt. Pour egg mixture over bread layers. Press bread into liquid. Let stand 10 minutes or until bread has absorbed liquid. Cover dish with buttered foil.

3. Pour 1 inch hot water into slow cooker. Add baking dish. Cover; cook on HIGH 3 hours or until toothpick inserted into center comes out clean. Remove dish and let stand 10 minutes to firm up. Dust with powdered sugar. Garnish with fresh fruit.   *Makes 6 servings*

Prep Time: 15 minutes
Cook Time: 3 hours

Chocolate-Stuffed Slow Cooker French Toast

simmering
soups & stews

Tofu and Snow Pea Noodle Bowl

  5 cups water
  6 tablespoons chicken or vegetarian broth powder*
  4 ounces uncooked vermicelli, broken in thirds
  ½ pound firm tofu, rinsed, patted dry and cut into ¼-inch cubes
  3 ounces snow peas, whole or slivered
  1 cup matchstick-size carrot strips**
  ½ teaspoon chili garlic sauce
  ½ cup chopped green onions
  ¼ cup chopped fresh cilantro (optional)
  2 tablespoons lime juice
  1 tablespoon grated fresh ginger
  2 teaspoons soy sauce

Vegetarian broth powder can be found in natural food stores and some supermarkets.

**Matchstick-size carrot strips are sometimes called shredded carrots and may be sold with other prepared vegetables in the supermarket produce section.*

1. Bring water to a boil in large saucepan over high heat. Stir in broth powder and vermicelli; return to a boil. Reduce heat to medium-high; simmer 6 minutes. Stir in tofu, snow peas, carrots and chili garlic sauce; simmer 2 minutes.

2. Remove from heat; stir in green onions, cilantro, if desired, lime juice, ginger and soy sauce. Serve immediately.

Makes 4 servings

Tip: Substitute 5 cups chicken or vegetable broth for the water and broth powder.

Chocolate Chili

- 2 tablespoons olive oil
- 1 onion, diced
- 1 teaspoon POLANER® Chopped Garlic
- 2 pounds lean ground beef
- 1 can (4 ounces) ORTEGA® Diced Green Chiles
- 1 packet (1.25 ounces) ORTEGA® Taco Seasoning Mix
- 1 can (28 ounces) diced tomatoes
- 1 jar (16 ounces) ORTEGA® Thick & Chunky Salsa
- 2 cups water
- ½ cup semisweet chocolate chips
- ½ cup slivered almonds
- 1 teaspoon ground cinnamon
- 1 can (15 ounces) pinto beans, drained

Heat oil over medium heat in large pot until hot. Add onion and garlic. Cook and stir until onions are tender, about 3 minutes.

Add beef, chiles and seasoning mix. Cook and stir about 5 minutes or until meat is browned.

Stir in tomatoes, salsa, water, chocolate chips, almonds and cinnamon. Bring to a boil. Reduce heat to low.

Simmer 45 minutes, stirring every 15 minutes. Add beans; heat 15 minutes longer or until beans are heated through.

Makes 8 servings

Serving Suggestion: Garnish with crumbled taco shells, shredded Cheddar cheese, cilantro and diced tomatoes.

Prep Time: 15 minutes
Start to Finish: 1½ hours

Chocolate Chili

Nancy's Chicken Noodle Soup

- 1 can (about 48 ounces) chicken broth
- 4 cups water
- 2 boneless skinless chicken breasts, cut into bite-size pieces
- ⅔ cup diced onion
- ⅔ cup diced celery
- ⅔ cup diced carrots
- ⅔ cup sliced mushrooms
- ½ cup frozen peas
- 4 chicken bouillon cubes
- 2 tablespoons butter
- 1 tablespoon dried parsley
- 1 teaspoon salt
- 1 teaspoon ground cumin
- 1 teaspoon dried marjoram
- 1 teaspoon black pepper
- 2 cups cooked egg noodles

Slow Cooker Directions

1. Combine all ingredients except noodles in 5-quart slow cooker.

2. Cover; cook on LOW 5 to 7 hours or on HIGH 3 to 4 hours. Stir in noodles 30 minutes before serving. *Makes 4 servings*

note

This is the perfect recipe to make during the week. Get it started before work and go. You'll have a comforting meal waiting when you get home.

Nancy's Chicken Noodle Soup

Retro Beef and Veggie Soup

    3 teaspoons olive oil, divided
  12 ounces boneless beef top sirloin, cut into bite-size pieces
    2 medium carrots, quartered lengthwise and cut into 2-inch pieces
    1 medium green bell pepper, coarsely chopped
    6 ounces green beans, cut into 2-inch pieces
    1 can (about 14 ounces) Italian-style stewed tomatoes
    1 cup beef broth
    8 ounces new potatoes, cut into bite-size pieces
    3 teaspoons instant coffee granules, divided
    ¾ teaspoon salt
    ¼ teaspoon black pepper

1. Heat 1 teaspoon oil in Dutch oven over medium-high heat. Brown beef 1 to 2 minutes; remove to plate.

2. Add remaining 2 teaspoons oil, carrots, bell pepper and green beans to Dutch oven. Cook and stir 4 minutes or until edges begin to brown. Add tomatoes, broth, potatoes and 1 teaspoon coffee granules; bring to a boil. Reduce heat. Add beef; cover and simmer 20 minutes or until potatoes are tender, stirring frequently.

3. Remove from heat. Add remaining 2 teaspoons coffee granules, salt and black pepper; stir well. *Makes 4 servings*

Retro Beef and Veggie Soup

Portuguese Potato & Greens Soup

2 tablespoons olive oil
1 cup chopped onion
1 cup chopped carrots
2 cloves garlic, minced
1 pound new red potatoes, cut into 1-inch pieces
2 cups water
1 can (about 14 ounces) chicken broth
¼ teaspoon salt
½ pound chorizo sausage, casings removed
½ pound kale, stems removed and sliced
  Additional salt
  Black pepper

1. Heat oil in large saucepan over medium heat. Add onion, carrots and garlic; cook and stir 5 to 6 minutes or until lightly browned. Add potatoes, water, broth and ¼ teaspoon salt; bring to a boil. Reduce heat to low; cover and simmer 10 to 15 minutes or until potatoes are tender. Cool slightly.

2. Meanwhile, heat large nonstick skillet over medium heat. Crumble chorizo into skillet. Cook and stir 5 to 6 minutes or until sausage is cooked through. Drain sausage on paper towels.

3. Add sausage and kale to broth mixture; cook, uncovered, 4 to 5 minutes over medium heat until heated through. Kale should be bright green and slightly crunchy. Season to taste with additional salt and pepper.

Makes 4 servings

Portuguese Potato & Greens Soup

Russian Borscht

4 cups thinly sliced green cabbage
1½ pounds fresh beets, shredded
5 small carrots, halved lengthwise and cut into 1-inch pieces
1 parsnip, peeled, halved lengthwise and cut into 1-inch pieces
1 cup chopped onion
4 cloves garlic, minced
1 pound beef stew meat, cut into ½-inch cubes
1 can (about 14 ounces) diced tomatoes
3 cans (about 14 ounces each) reduced-sodium beef broth
¼ cup lemon juice
1 tablespoon sugar
1 teaspoon black pepper
Additional lemon juice and sugar (optional)
Sour cream (optional)
Fresh parsley (optional)

Slow Cooker Directions

1. Layer cabbage, beets, carrots, parsnip, onion, garlic, beef, tomatoes, broth, lemon juice, sugar and pepper in slow cooker. Cover; cook on LOW 7 to 9 hours or until vegetables are crisp-tender.

2. Season with additional lemon juice and sugar, if desired. Dollop with sour cream and sprinkle with parsley, if desired.

Makes 12 servings

Russian Borscht

New Orleans Fish Soup

- 1 can (about 15 ounces) cannellini beans, rinsed and drained
- 1 can (about 14 ounces) reduced-sodium chicken broth
- 1 small yellow summer squash, halved lengthwise and sliced
- 1 tablespoon Cajun seasoning
- 2 cans (about 14 ounces each) no-salt-added stewed tomatoes, undrained
- 1 pound skinless firm fish fillets, such as grouper, cod or haddock, cut into 1-inch pieces
- ½ cup sliced green onions
- 1 teaspoon grated orange peel

1. Combine beans, broth, squash and Cajun seasoning in large saucepan. Bring to a boil. Reduce heat; cover and simmer 5 minutes.

2. Stir in tomatoes with juice and fish. Bring to a boil. Reduce heat; cover and gently simmer 3 to 5 minutes or until fish is opaque and begins to flake when tested with fork. Stir in green onions and orange peel.   *Makes 4 servings*

note

Cannellini beans are large white Italian kidney beans. They make a great addition to salads, soups and stews.

New Orleans Fish Soup

Chicken and Sausage Gumbo with Beer

½ cup all-purpose flour
½ cup vegetable oil
4½ cups chicken broth
1 bottle (12 ounces) beer
3 pounds boneless skinless chicken thighs, cut into pieces
½ teaspoon salt
½ teaspoon garlic powder
¾ teaspoon ground red pepper, divided
1 pound fully cooked andouille sausage, sliced into rounds
1 large onion, chopped
½ red bell pepper, chopped
½ green bell pepper, chopped
2 stalks celery, chopped
2 cloves garlic, minced
2 bay leaves
1 teaspoon salt
½ teaspoon black pepper
3 cups hot cooked rice
½ cup sliced green onions

1. Stir together flour and oil in large saucepan or Dutch oven. Cook and stir over medium-low heat until mixture is the color of chocolate, about 1 hour. (Once mixture begins to darken, watch carefully to avoid burning.)

2. Heat broth and beer in medium saucepan to a simmer; keep warm over low heat. Season chicken with salt, garlic powder and ¼ teaspoon red pepper.

3. Add chicken, sausage, onion, bell peppers, celery, garlic, bay leaves, salt, black pepper and remaining ½ teaspoon red pepper to flour mixture; stir well. Gradually add hot chicken broth mixture, stirring well after each addition to prevent lumps. Bring to a simmer. Cover and simmer over low heat 1 to 2 hours. Remove and discard bay leaves. Spoon ½ cup rice into bowls; top with gumbo. Sprinkle with green onions before serving. *Makes 6 servings*

Hungarian Beef Goulash

¼ cup all-purpose flour
1 tablespoon Hungarian sweet paprika
1½ teaspoons salt
½ teaspoon Hungarian hot paprika
½ teaspoon black pepper
2 pounds beef stew meat
¼ cup vegetable oil, divided
1 large onion, chopped
4 cloves garlic, minced
2 cans (about 14 ounces each) beef broth
1 can (about 14 ounces) stewed tomatoes, undrained
1 cup water
1 tablespoon dried marjoram
3 cups uncooked thin egg noodles
1 large green bell pepper, chopped
Sour cream

1. Combine flour, sweet paprika, salt, hot paprika and black pepper in large resealable food storage bag. Add half of beef. Seal bag; shake to coat well. Remove beef; set aside. Repeat with remaining beef.

2. Heat 4½ teaspoons oil in Dutch oven over medium heat. Add half of beef; brown on all sides. Transfer to large bowl. Repeat with 4½ teaspoons oil and remaining beef; transfer to same bowl.

3. Heat remaining 1 tablespoon oil in same Dutch oven. Add onion and garlic; cook 8 minutes or until tender, stirring often.

4. Return beef and any accumulated juices to Dutch oven. Add broth, tomatoes with juice, water and marjoram. Bring to a boil over medium-high heat. Reduce heat; cover and simmer 1½ hours or until meat is tender, stirring once.

5. Stir in noodles and bell pepper; cover and simmer about 8 minutes or until noodles are tender, stirring once. Ladle into soup bowls; top with sour cream. *Makes 8 servings*

Vegetable and Red Lentil Soup

1 can (about 14 ounces) vegetable broth
1 can (about 14 ounces) diced tomatoes
2 medium zucchini or yellow summer squash (or 1 of each), diced
1 red or yellow bell pepper, diced
½ cup thinly sliced carrots
½ cup red lentils,* rinsed and sorted
½ teaspoon salt
½ teaspoon sugar
¼ teaspoon black pepper
2 tablespoons chopped fresh basil or thyme
½ cup croutons or shredded cheese (optional)

Substitute brown lentils if red lentils are unavailable.

Slow Cooker Directions

1. Combine broth, tomatoes, zucchini, bell pepper, carrots, lentils, salt, sugar and black pepper in slow cooker. Cover; cook on LOW 8 hours or on HIGH 4 hours.

2. Ladle into bowls; top with basil and croutons, if desired.

Makes 4 servings

Fruited Lamb Stew

1 pound boneless lamb
2 tablespoons all-purpose flour
½ teaspoon salt
   Dash ground red pepper
2 tablespoons vegetable oil
3 cups chicken broth
1 small leek, sliced
½ teaspoon grated fresh ginger
8 ounces baby carrots
¾ cup chopped mixed dried fruit (half of 8-ounce package)
½ cup frozen peas
   Black pepper
1⅓ cups hot cooked couscous

continued on page 52

Vegetable and Red Lentil Soup

Fruited Lamb Stew, continued

1. Preheat oven to 350°F. Cut lamb into ¾-inch cubes. Combine flour, salt and red pepper in medium bowl. Add lamb; toss to coat with flour mixture.

2. Heat oil in 5-quart ovenproof Dutch oven over medium-high heat. Add lamb; brown on all sides, stirring frequently. Add broth, leek and ginger to Dutch oven. Bring to a boil over high heat. Cover; bake in oven 45 minutes.

3. Stir in carrots. Cover; bake 30 minutes or until meat and carrots are almost tender.

4. Stir fruit and peas into stew. Cover; bake 10 minutes. Skim off fat, if necessary. Season with black pepper. Serve stew in bowls; top with couscous. *Makes 4 servings*

Stew Provençal

  2 cans (about 14 ounces each) beef broth, divided
  ⅓ cup all-purpose flour
  1 to 2 pork tenderloins (about 2 pounds), trimmed and diced
  4 red potatoes, unpeeled, cut into cubes
  2 cups frozen cut green beans, thawed
  1 onion, chopped
  2 cloves garlic, minced
  1 teaspoon salt
  1 teaspoon dried thyme
  ½ teaspoon black pepper

Slow Cooker Directions

1. Combine ¾ cup beef broth and flour in small bowl. Cover and refrigerate.

2. Add remaining broth, pork, potatoes, beans, onion, garlic, salt, thyme and pepper to slow cooker; mix well.

3. Cover; cook on LOW 8 to 10 hours or on HIGH 4 to 5 hours. Stir flour mixture into slow cooker. Cook, uncovered, 30 minutes or until thickened. *Makes 8 servings*

Stew Provençal

Country Sausage and Bean Soup

    2 cans (about 14 ounces each) reduced-sodium chicken broth
1½ cups hot water
    1 cup dried black beans, rinsed and sorted
    1 cup chopped yellow onion
    2 bay leaves
    1 teaspoon sugar
  ⅛ teaspoon ground red pepper
     Nonstick cooking spray
    6 ounces bulk pork sausage
    1 cup chopped tomato
    1 tablespoon chili powder
    1 tablespoon Worcestershire sauce
    2 teaspoons olive oil
1½ teaspoons ground cumin
  ½ teaspoon salt
  ¼ cup chopped fresh cilantro

Slow Cooker Directions

1. Combine broth, water, beans, onion, bay leaves, sugar and red pepper in slow cooker. Cover; cook on HIGH 4 hours or on LOW 8 hours.

2. Coat large nonstick skillet with cooking spray. Brown sausage over medium-high heat 6 to 8 minutes, stirring to break up meat. Drain fat.

3. Add sausage, tomato, chili powder, Worcestershire sauce, oil, cumin and salt to slow cooker. Cover; cook on HIGH 15 minutes. Remove and discard bay leaves. Top with cilantro before serving.

Makes 9 servings

Country Sausage and Bean Soup

Smokey Chili with Pasta

    2 cups (about 6 ounces) rotelle or rotini pasta, uncooked
    1 pound ground beef
    1 cup chopped onion
    2 cans (about 15 ounces each) red kidney beans
    2 cans (10¾ ounces each) condensed tomato soup
    2 tablespoons HERSHEY₅'S Cocoa
2¼ teaspoons chili powder
  ¾ teaspoon ground black pepper
  ½ teaspoon salt
      Grated Parmesan cheese (optional)

1. Cook pasta according to package directions; drain.

2. Meanwhile, cook ground beef and onion until meat is thoroughly done and onion is tender. If necessary, drain fat.

3. Stir in undrained kidney beans, soup, cocoa, chili powder, pepper and salt. Heat to boiling; reduce heat. Stir in hot pasta; heat thoroughly. Serve with Parmesan cheese, if desired.

Makes 8 servings

New England Clam Chowder

    1 cup salt
  24 medium fresh clams
    1 bottle (8 ounces) clam juice
    3 medium potatoes, cut into ½-inch-thick slices
  ¼ teaspoon dried thyme
  ¼ teaspoon white pepper
    4 slices bacon, cut crosswise into ¼-inch strips
    1 medium onion, chopped
  ⅓ cup all-purpose flour
    2 cups milk
    1 cup half-and-half

1. Combine 1 gallon water and ⅓ cup in stockpot or clean bucket. Scrub clams with stiff brush. Soak in salt water 20 minutes. Drain; repeat 2 more times. Refrigerate clams 1 hour.

continued on page 58

Smokey Chili with Pasta

New England Clam Chowder, continued

2. Shuck clams, reserving juice. Strain fresh clam juice through triple thickness of dampened cheesecloth; pour into 2-cup glass measure. Refrigerate until needed. Coarsely chop clams; set aside.

3. Add bottled clam juice and enough water to fresh clam juice in glass measure to make 2 cups liquid; place liquid in Dutch oven. Add potatoes, thyme and pepper; bring to a boil. Reduce heat; simmer 15 minutes or until potatoes are tender, stirring occasionally.

4. Meanwhile, cook bacon in large skillet over medium heat until almost crisp. Add onion; cook until tender but not brown. Stir flour into bacon mixture. Whisk in milk; cook and stir until mixture boils and thickens.

5. Add bacon mixture and half-and-half to potato mixture. Add clams; continue to cook until clams are firm.   *Makes 6 servings*

Slow Cooker Veggie Stew

  1 **tablespoon vegetable oil**
  ⅔ **cup carrot slices**
  ½ **cup diced onion**
  2 **cloves garlic, chopped**
  2 **cans (about 14 ounces each) vegetable broth**
1½ **cups chopped green cabbage**
  ½ **cup cut green beans**
  ½ **cup diced zucchini**
  1 **tablespoon tomato paste**
  ½ **teaspoon dried basil**
  ½ **teaspoon dried oregano**
  ¼ **teaspoon salt**

Slow Cooker Directions

1. Heat oil in medium skillet over medium-high heat. Add carrot, onion and garlic. Cook and stir until tender.

2. Place carrot mixture and remaining ingredients in slow cooker; stir to combine. Cover; cook on LOW 8 to 10 hours or on HIGH 4 to 5 hours.   *Makes 4 to 6 servings*

Slow Cooker Veggie Stew

Coconut Curry Chicken Soup

3 cups chicken broth
8 boneless skinless chicken thighs
1 cup chopped onion, divided
1 teaspoon salt, divided
4 whole cloves
1 tablespoon butter
2 tablespoons curry powder
1¼ cups coconut milk
5 tablespoons chopped fresh mint, divided
3 tablespoons crystallized ginger
¼ teaspoon ground cloves
1½ cups half-and-half
3 cups hot cooked rice
Lime wedges (optional)

1. Bring broth to a boil in large skillet over high heat. Add chicken, ½ cup onion, ½ teaspoon salt and whole cloves. Return to a boil. Reduce heat; cover tightly and simmer 40 minutes or until chicken is very tender.

2. Remove chicken; set aside. Reserve 1 cup broth; discard remaining broth and vegetables. Increase heat to medium-high; melt butter in skillet. Add remaining ½ cup onion; cook and stir about 4 minutes or until onion is translucent. Sprinkle curry powder over onions; cook and stir constantly just until fragrant, about 20 seconds.

3. Add coconut milk, 1 tablespoon mint, ginger, ground cloves and reserved 1 cup broth to skillet; cover and simmer 10 minutes. Add chicken to coconut mixture; cover and simmer 15 minutes. Stir in half-and-half and remaining ½ teaspoon salt. Shred chicken slightly, pressing down with a spoon. Cook 1 minute longer or until heated through. Top with remaining mint and rice. Garnish with lime wedges. *Makes 4 servings*

Coconut Curry Chicken Soup

Chunky Italian Stew with White Beans

   1 teaspoon olive oil
   2 green bell peppers, cut into ¾-inch pieces
   1 yellow squash,* cut into ¾-inch pieces
   1 zucchini,* cut into ¾-inch pieces
   1 onion, cut into ¾-inch pieces
   4 ounces whole mushrooms, quartered (about 1 cup)
   1 can (about 14 ounces) reduced-sodium diced tomatoes
   1 teaspoon dried oregano
   ½ teaspoon sugar
   ½ teaspoon Italian seasoning
   ⅛ teaspoon red pepper flakes (optional)
   1 can (about 15 ounces) reduced-sodium navy beans, rinsed and
      drained
   ¾ cup (3 ounces) shredded mozzarella cheese
   1 tablespoon grated Parmesan cheese

Or, use 2 zucchini or 2 yellow squash instead of 1 each, if desired.

1. Heat oil in Dutch oven or large saucepan over medium-high heat. Add bell peppers, yellow squash, zucchini, onion and mushrooms. Cook and stir 8 minutes or until onions are translucent.

2. Add tomatoes, oregano, sugar, Italian seasoning and red pepper flakes, if desired. Reduce heat; cover and simmer 15 minutes or until vegetables are tender, stirring once.

3. Remove Dutch oven from heat. Stir in beans; let stand, covered, 5 minutes. Spoon into 4 bowls; sprinkle with cheeses.

Makes 4 servings

Chunky Italian Stew with White Beans

sizzling skillet meals

Polka Dot Lasagna Skillet

  1 pound ground turkey or beef
  1 package lasagna and sauce meal kit
  4 cups hot water
  ½ cup ricotta cheese
  1 egg
  3 tablespoons grated Parmesan cheese
  2 tablespoons all-purpose flour
  2 tablespoons chopped fresh parsley
  ½ teaspoon Italian seasoning
  ¼ teaspoon black pepper

1. Brown turkey in large skillet over medium-high heat 6 to 8 minutes, stirring to break up meat. Drain fat.

2. Stir in contents of meal kit and hot water; bring to a boil. Reduce heat to low; cover and cook 10 minutes.

3. Meanwhile, blend ricotta cheese, egg, Parmesan cheese, flour, parsley, Italian seasoning and pepper in small bowl until smooth. Drop tablespoonfuls of ricotta mixture over pasta; cover and cook 4 to 5 minutes or until dumplings are set. Remove from heat; let stand about 4 minutes before serving.   *Makes 4 to 6 servings*

Chicken with Rice & Asparagus Pilaf

　4 boneless skinless chicken breasts
　3 teaspoons poultry seasoning, divided
　2 tablespoons olive oil
　1 medium onion, chopped
　1 cup uncooked rice
　1 clove garlic, minced
　2 cups chicken broth
　¾ teaspoon salt
　1 pound asparagus, trimmed and cut into 2-inch pieces (about
　　　3 cups)

1. Sprinkle each chicken breast with ¼ teaspoon poultry seasoning. Heat oil in large skillet over medium-high heat. Brown chicken about 2 minutes on each side. Remove from skillet.

2. Add onion; cook and stir 3 minutes. Add rice and garlic; cook and stir 1 to 2 minutes. Add broth, remaining 2 teaspoons poultry seasoning and salt. Bring to a boil over high heat. Reduce heat to low; cook, covered, 5 minutes.

3. Stir in asparagus; add chicken. Cover; cook 10 to 12 minutes or until rice is tender and chicken is cooked through (165°F).

Makes 4 servings

Hoppin' John

　1 package (14 ounces) smoked turkey sausage, thinly sliced
　3 cans (15½ ounces each) black-eyed peas, drained, rinsed
　2 cans (14½ ounces each) chicken broth
　2 cups chopped onion
　1 teaspoon crushed red pepper
　½ teaspoon ground red pepper
2½ cups MINUTE® White Rice, uncooked
　　Chopped fresh parsley (optional)

Brown sausage in medium saucepan over medium-high heat. Add peas, broth, onions and seasonings; bring to a boil. Stir in rice; cover. Simmer 10 minutes or until rice is tender. Garnish with parsley, if desired. *Makes 8 servings*

Chicken with Rice & Asparagus Pilaf

Spicy Italian Sausage & Penne Pasta

- **8 ounces uncooked penne pasta**
- **1 pound bulk hot Italian sausage**
- **1 cup chopped sweet onion**
- **2 cloves garlic, minced**
- **2 cans (about 14 ounces each) diced tomatoes**
- **3 cups broccoli florets**
- **½ cup shredded Asiago or Romano cheese**

1. Cook pasta according to package directions; drain. Return to saucepan; keep warm.

2. Meanwhile, crumble sausage into large skillet. Add onion. Cook over medium-high heat until sausage is no longer pink, stirring to break up meat. Drain fat. Add garlic; cook 1 minute. Stir in tomatoes and broccoli. Cover; cook 10 minutes or until broccoli is tender.

3. Add sausage mixture to pasta; toss well. Sprinkle with cheese.

Makes 4 to 6 servings

note

To add extra flavor to pasta dishes, slice fresh basil leaves into thin shreds. Sprinkle over hot pasta just before serving.

Spicy Italian Sausage & Penne Pasta

Thai Basil Pork Stir-Fry

1 pound boneless pork tenderloin, sliced across the grain into ¼-inch slices

1 tablespoon soy sauce

½ teaspoon crushed or minced garlic

2 tablespoons canola oil

3 cups broccoli florets

1 medium red bell pepper, cut into strips

1 to 2 tablespoons Thai green curry paste*

1¼ cups chicken broth

2 tablespoons chopped basil

3 cups fresh mung bean sprouts

2 tablespoons finely chopped roasted peanuts

Thai green curry paste is available in the ethnic section of most supermarkets in cans or jars. Use 1 tablespoon for a mildly spicy dish or 2 tablespoons for a hot dish.

1. Combine pork, soy sauce and garlic in small bowl; toss to coat. Set aside.

2. Heat oil in large nonstick skillet over high heat. Add broccoli; stir-fry 3 to 4 minutes or until broccoli begins to brown but is not cooked through. Add bell pepper; stir-fry 1 minute. Add reserved pork mixture and curry paste; stir-fry 2 minutes. Add broth; cook and stir 2 to 3 minutes or until heated through.

3. Remove from heat; stir in basil. Serve with bean sprouts; sprinkle each serving with chopped peanuts.   *Makes 6 servings*

Thai Basil Pork Stir-Fry

Creamy Fettuccine with Asparagus & Lima Beans

8 ounces uncooked fettuccine
2 tablespoons butter
2 cups fresh asparagus pieces (about 1 inch long)
1 cup frozen lima beans, thawed
¼ teaspoon black pepper
½ cup chicken or vegetable broth
1 cup half-and-half or whipping cream
1 cup (4 ounces) grated Parmesan cheese

1. Cook fettuccine according to package directions. Drain well; cover and keep warm.

2. Meanwhile, melt butter in large skillet over medium-high heat. Add asparagus, lima beans and pepper; cook and stir 3 minutes. Add broth; simmer 3 minutes. Add half-and-half; simmer 3 to 4 minutes or until vegetables are tender.

3. Add vegetable mixture and cheese to fettuccine; toss well. Serve immediately. *Makes 4 servings*

Skillet Pizza

2 cups MINUTE® White or Brown Rice, uncooked
1 package (5 ounces) pepperoni slices
1 jar (14 ounces) pizza sauce
1½ cups (6 ounces) shredded mozzarella cheese, divided
1 can (2.25 ounces) sliced black olives, drained (optional)

Prepare rice according to package directions. Combine rice, pepperoni, sauce, 1 cup cheese and olives, if desired, in large skillet over medium heat. Cook and stir until thoroughly heated. Top with remaining cheese before serving. *Makes 4 servings*

Tip: Add mushrooms, green olives, sausage or Canadian bacon. (If using fresh mushrooms, cook and stir in hot skillet before adding rice and remaining ingredients.)

Creamy Fettuccine with Asparagus & Lima Beans

Ham and Swiss Penne Skillet

2 ounces bread, torn into small pieces
5 tablespoons butter, divided
1 teaspoon salt, divided
½ teaspoon black pepper, divided
4 cups water
6 ounces uncooked penne pasta
3 tablespoons all-purpose flour
2¾ cups whole milk
1 cup (4 ounces) shredded Swiss cheese
6 ounces ham, diced
1 cup frozen corn, thawed
¾ cup frozen peas, thawed
½ cup finely chopped green onions

1. Place bread in food processor and pulse until coarse crumbs form.

2. Melt 2 tablespoons butter in large skillet over medium heat, tilting skillet to coat evenly. Add bread crumbs, ¼ teaspoon salt and ¼ teaspoon pepper. Cook and stir 2 to 3 minutes or until golden. Transfer to plate; set aside.

3. Add water to skillet and bring to a boil over high heat. Add pasta. Return to a boil; cook until just tender, stirring occasionally. Drain well; set aside.

4. Melt remaining 3 tablespoons butter in skillet over medium heat. Add flour; whisk until smooth. Add milk; whisk until well blended. Cook and stir 3 to 4 minutes or until slightly thickened, using flat spatula to scrape sides and bottom. Add cooked pasta, cheese, ham, corn, peas and green onions. Stir gently to blend well; cook 3 to 4 minutes or until thickened slightly. Remove from heat and top evenly with bread crumbs.   *Makes 4 servings*

Ham and Swiss Penne Skillet

30-Minute Paella

   2 tablespoons olive oil
   1 package (about 10 ounces) chicken-flavored rice and
      vermicelli mix
   ¼ teaspoon red pepper flakes
   3½ cups water
   1 package (about 10 ounces) refrigerated fully cooked chicken
      breast strips, cut into ½-inch pieces
   1 package (8 ounces) medium raw shrimp, peeled
   1 cup frozen peas
   ¼ cup diced roasted red pepper

1. Heat oil in large skillet over medium heat. Add vermicelli mix and red pepper flakes; cook and stir 2 minutes or until vermicelli is golden.

2. Add water, chicken, shrimp, peas, roasted red pepper and seasoning packet; bring to a boil. Reduce heat to low. Cover; cook 12 to 15 minutes or until rice is tender, stirring occasionally.

Makes 6 servings

note

The Spanish dish, paella, is named after the pan in which it is traditionally cooked and served. Recipes feature a variety of combinations of meats, seafood and vegetables.

30-Minute Paella

Chicken & Stuffing Skillet

3 tablespoons butter
1½ pounds skinless, boneless chicken breast halves (about 4 to 6)
1 box (6 ounces) Pepperidge Farm® One Step Chicken Flavored Stuffing Mix
1¼ cups water
1 can (10¾ ounces) Campbell's® Condensed Cream of Mushroom Soup (Regular *or* 98% Fat Free)
½ cup milk
½ cup shredded Cheddar cheese

1. Heat **1 tablespoon** butter in a 10-inch skillet over medium-high heat. Add the chicken and cook for 12 to 15 minutes or until the chicken is cooked through.* Remove the chicken and set it aside.

2. Prepare the stuffing in the skillet using the water and the remaining butter according to the package directions **except** let it stand for 2 minutes.

3. Return the chicken to the skillet and reduce the heat to medium. Stir the soup and milk in a small bowl and pour it over the chicken. Sprinkle with the cheese. Cover and cook until the mixture is hot and bubbling. *Makes 6 servings*

The internal temperature of the chicken should reach 160°F.

Start to Finish Time: 25 minutes
Prep Time: 5 minutes
Cook Time: 20 minutes

Couscous With Lamb and Olives

    1 tablespoon olive oil
1 1/4 pound boneless lamb stew meat, cut into 1-inch chunks
    1/2 teaspoon kosher salt
    1/2 teaspoon hot paprika
    1/4 cup (1 ounce) quartered garlic cloves
    3 cups brown stock
    1/3 cup red wine
    1/4 cup dried currants
    2 cups diced carrots (1-inch)
    1 cup California Ripe Olives, whole, pitted
1 1/3 cups Israeli couscous
    1/4 cup chopped parsley

Heat oil in a large sauce pot or braising pan over medium high heat. Add lamb, season with salt and paprika and cook for 5 to 6 minutes, stirring occasionally until browned on all sides. Stir in garlic and continue cooking for 2 to 3 minutes until golden. Pour in stock, wine and currants and bring to a boil. Turn heat down to a simmer and cook, covered, for one hour. Add carrots and California Ripe Olives and cook, covered, for 30 minutes. Uncover, stir in couscous and parsley and cook for 15 more minutes until couscous is tender. Serve immediately.   *Makes 4 servings*

Favorite recipe from **California Olive Industry**

Udon Noodles with Chicken & Spinach

3 tablespoons vegetable oil, divided

4 boneless skinless chicken thighs (about 12 ounces), cut into bite-size pieces

2 to 3 teaspoons grated fresh ginger

2 cloves garlic, minced

1 cup chicken broth

6 cups (6 ounces) coarsely chopped baby spinach

2 green onions, chopped

1 package (8 ounces) udon noodles, cooked and drained

1 tablespoon soy sauce

1. Heat 2 tablespoons oil in large nonstick skillet over medium heat. Add chicken; cook and stir 2 to 3 minutes or until cooked through. Remove and drain on paper towels.

2. Add remaining 1 tablespoon oil to skillet. Add ginger and garlic; cook over low heat 20 seconds or until garlic begins to color. Add chicken broth; bring to a simmer. Stir in spinach and green onions. Cook 2 to 3 minutes or until spinach wilts.

3. Stir chicken, noodles and soy sauce into spinach mixture. Serve immediately. *Makes 4 to 6 servings*

Broccoli Chicken Potato Parmesan

2 tablespoons vegetable oil

1 pound small red potatoes, sliced ¼ inch thick

1 can (10 ¾ ounces) Campbell's® Condensed Broccoli Cheese Soup (Regular *or* 98% Fat Free)

½ cup milk

¼ teaspoon garlic powder

2 cups fresh *or* frozen broccoli flowerets

1 package (about 10 ounces) refrigerated cooked chicken breast strips

¼ cup grated Parmesan cheese

continued on page 82

Udon Noodles with Chicken & Spinach

Broccoli Chicken Potato Parmesan, continued

1. Heat the oil in a 10-inch skillet over medium heat. Add the potatoes. Cover and cook for 10 minutes, stirring occasionally.

2. Stir the soup, milk, garlic powder, broccoli and chicken into the skillet. Sprinkle with cheese. Heat to a boil. Reduce heat to low. Cover and cook for 5 minutes or until potatoes are fork-tender.

Makes 4 servings

Beef and Asparagus Stir-Fry

¾ **cup water**
3 **tablespoons soy sauce**
3 **tablespoons hoisin sauce**
1 **tablespoon cornstarch**
1 **tablespoon peanut or vegetable oil**
1 **pound sirloin steak, cut into thin strips**
1 **teaspoon dark sesame oil**
8 **shiitake mushrooms, stems removed and thinly sliced**
1 **cup baby corn**
8 **ounces asparagus (8 to 10 medium spears), cut into 1-inch pieces**
1 **cup sugar snap peas or snow peas**
½ **cup red bell pepper strips**
½ **cup cherry tomato halves (optional)**

1. Whisk together water, soy sauce, hoisin sauce and cornstarch in small bowl; set aside.

2. Heat peanut oil in large skillet or wok over medium-high heat. Add beef; cook and stir 5 to 6 minutes or until still slightly pink. Remove beef to plate with slotted spoon.

3. Add sesame oil, mushrooms and baby corn to skillet; cook and stir 2 to 3 minutes or until mushrooms are tender and corn is heated through. Add asparagus, snap peas and peppers; cook and stir 1 minute or until crisp-tender.

4. Return beef with any juices to skillet. Stir reserved soy sauce mixture and add to skillet; add tomatoes, if desired. Cook and stir 1 minute or until heated through and sauce thickens.

Makes 4 servings

Beef and Asparagus Stir-Fry

Teriyaki Steak and Brown Rice Dinner

    1 tablespoon vegetable oil
    1 pound boneless beef sirloin steak, cut into strips*
    1 teaspoon garlic powder
    2 cups water
  ⅓ cup teriyaki sauce**
    2 cups MINUTE® Brown Rice, uncooked
    4 cups broccoli florets
    1 large red bell pepper, cut into strips

*Or substitute 1 pound boneless skinless chicken breasts, cut into strips.

**Or substitute ¼ cup soy sauce plus 2 tablespoons water.

Heat oil in large nonstick skillet over medium-high heat. Sprinkle steak with garlic powder. Add to skillet; cook and stir 5 minutes or until steak is cooked through. Stir in water and teriyaki sauce; bring to a boil. Stir in rice, broccoli and bell pepper. Return to a boil. Reduce heat to low; cover. Simmer 5 minutes. Remove from heat. Let stand 5 minutes. Fluff with fork.   *Makes 4 servings*

Italian Veg•All® Skillet

    1 pound ground beef
    1 can (15 ounces) VEG•ALL® Original Mixed Vegetables, drained
    1 jar (15½ ounces) prepared spaghetti sauce
    8 ounces uncooked pasta shells
    1 cup water
    1 cup tomato or vegetable juice
  ½ cup chopped onion
    1 tablespoon chopped parsley
  ½ teaspoon oregano
  ½ cup shredded Cheddar cheese

In large skillet, brown ground beef; drain thoroughly.

Add remaining ingredients except cheese. Bring to a boil. Cover; reduce heat and simmer 20 minutes, stirring occasionally.

Top with cheese. Cover; remove from heat. Cool 5 minutes or until cheese melts.   *Makes 4 to 6 servings*

Teriyaki Steak and Brown Rice Dinner

Homestyle Skillet Chicken

  1 tablespoon Cajun seasoning
  ½ teaspoon plus ⅛ teaspoon black pepper, divided
  ½ teaspoon salt, divided
  4 chicken thighs
  2 tablespoons vegetable oil
  4 cloves garlic, minced
  8 small red or new potatoes, quartered
12 pearl onions, peeled*
  1 cup baby carrots
  2 stalks celery, halved lengthwise and sliced diagonally into ½-inch pieces
  ½ red bell pepper, diced
  2 tablespoons all-purpose flour
  1 cup reduced-sodium chicken broth
  ½ cup sherry
  2 tablespoons finely chopped fresh parsley

To peel pearl onions, drop into boiling water for 30 seconds, then plunge immediately into ice water. The peel should slide right off.

1. Combine Cajun seasoning, ½ teaspoon black pepper and ¼ teaspoon salt in small bowl. Rub mixture onto all sides of chicken.

2. Heat oil in large heavy skillet over medium-high heat. Add garlic and chicken; cook about 3 minutes per side or until chicken is browned. Transfer chicken to plate; set aside.

3. Add potatoes, onions, carrots, celery and bell pepper to skillet; cook and stir 3 minutes. Sprinkle flour over vegetables; stir to coat. Slowly stir in broth and sherry, scraping up browned bits from bottom of skillet. Bring mixture to a boil, stirring constantly.

4. Reduce heat to medium-low. Return chicken to skillet. Cover and cook about 30 minutes or until juices of chicken run clear. Increase heat to medium-high; cook, uncovered, about 5 minutes or until sauce is thickened.

5. Season with remaining ¼ teaspoon salt and ⅛ teaspoon black pepper. Sprinkle with parsley. *Makes 4 servings*

Homestyle Skillet Chicken

Luscious Lo Mein

- 8 ounces uncooked lo mein or udon noodles or spaghetti
- 2 tablespoons vegetable oil
- 1 package JENNIE-O TURKEY STORE® Boneless Breast Tenderloins, cut into ¾-inch chunks
- 2 teaspoons bottled or fresh minced ginger
- 2 teaspoons bottled or fresh minced garlic
- ¼ teaspoon crushed red pepper flakes
- 2 cups sliced bok choy or fresh sugar snap peas
- 1 cup thin red bell pepper strips
- ¼ cup chicken broth
- ¼ cup soy sauce or tamari
- 2 tablespoons oyster sauce
- 2 tablespoons dark sesame oil

Cook noodles according to package directions. Meanwhile, heat 1 tablespoon vegetable oil in large deep skillet over medium-high heat. Add turkey, ginger, garlic and pepper flakes; stir-fry 3 minutes. Transfer to bowl; set aside. Add remaining 1 tablespoon vegetable oil to skillet. Add bok choy and bell pepper; stir-fry 2 minutes. Add broth, soy sauce and oyster sauce; bring to a simmer. Add turkey and sesame oil to skillet; simmer 2 minutes or until turkey is no longer pink in center. Drain noodles; add to skillet and heat through. Serve in shallow soup bowls. *Makes 6 servings*

Prep Time: 30 minutes
Cook Time: 15 minutes

Luscious Lo Mein

Cocoa Spiced Beef Stir-Fry

2 cups beef broth
3 tablespoons soy sauce
2 tablespoons cornstarch
2 tablespoons HERSHEY'S Cocoa
2 teaspoons minced garlic (about 4 cloves)
1½ teaspoons ground ginger
1 teaspoon crushed red pepper flakes
1 pound boneless beef top round or flank steak
3 tablespoons vegetable oil, divided
1½ cups large onion pieces
1 cup carrot slices
3 cups fresh broccoli florets and pieces
1½ cups sweet red pepper slices
Hot cooked rice
Additional soy sauce
Cashew or peanut pieces (optional)

1. Stir together beef broth, soy sauce, cornstarch, cocoa, garlic, ginger and red pepper flakes; set aside. Cut beef steak into ¼-inch-wide strips.

2. Heat large skillet or wok over high heat about 1 minute or until hot. Drizzle about 1 tablespoon oil into pan; heat about 30 seconds. Add beef strips; stir-fry until well browned. Remove from heat; set aside.

3. Drizzle remaining 2 tablespoons oil into pan; add onion pieces and carrots. Stir-fry until onion is crisp-tender. Add broccoli and red pepper strips; cook until crisp-tender.

4. Return beef to pan; add broth mixture. Cook and stir until mixture comes to a boil and thickens. Serve over hot rice with additional soy sauce and cashew pieces, if desired. *Makes 4 to 6 servings*

Cocoa Spiced Beef Stir-Fry

Crab and Scallion Quesadillas

8 ounces pasteurized crabmeat

¾ cup cream cheese, softened

4 green onions (white and green parts), diced

Zest of 1 lime

1 ORTEGA® Soft Taco Kit—includes 10 soft tortillas, 1 packet (1.25 ounces) taco seasoning mix and 1 packet (3 ounces) taco sauce

Nonstick cooking spray

1 tomato, diced

¼ cup chopped cilantro

½ cup sour cream

In mixing bowl, combine crabmeat, cream cheese, green onions, lime zest, and half of seasoning mix from Soft Taco Kit.

Heat large skillet over medium heat and spray with nonstick cooking spray. Spread about 1 teaspoon taco sauce onto flour tortilla from Soft Taco Kit. Spread about ¼ cup of crab mixture over sauce. Place tortilla-side down into hot skillet and top with another tortilla. Cook about 4 minutes or until bottom of tortilla is browned. Spray top tortilla with nonstick cooking spray and turn over. Cook another 4 minutes. Repeat with remaining quesadillas. (Cook 2 at a time if skillet is large enough.)

Cut quesadillas into quarters and top with tomato, cilantro and sour cream to serve. *Makes 5 servings*

Note: Place cooked quesadillas in preheated 200°F oven and cover to keep warm.

Prep Time: 10 minutes
Start to Finish: 20 minutes

Crab and Scallion Quesadillas

simply slow cooked

Sweet and Sour Shrimp

  1 can (16 ounces) sliced peaches in syrup, undrained
  ½ cup chopped green onions
  ½ cup chopped red bell pepper
  ½ cup chopped green bell pepper
  ½ cup chopped celery
  ⅓ cup vegetable broth
  ¼ cup soy sauce
  2 tablespoons rice wine vinegar
  2 tablespoons dark sesame oil
  1 teaspoon red pepper flakes
  1 package (6 ounces) snow peas
  1 pound medium cooked shrimp
  1 cup cherry tomatoes, halved
  ½ cup toasted walnut pieces
    Hot cooked rice

Slow Cooker Directions

1. Place peaches, onions, bell peppers, celery, broth, soy sauce, vinegar, sesame oil and pepper flakes in slow cooker. Cover; cook on LOW 3 to 4 hours or on HIGH 2 to 3 hours or until vegetables are tender. Stir well.

2. Add snow peas. Cover; cook on HIGH 15 minutes.

3. Add shrimp, tomatoes and walnuts. Cover; cook on HIGH 10 to 15 minutes or until shrimp is hot. Serve with rice.

Makes 4 to 6 servings

Prep Time: 15 to 20 minutes
Cook Time: 3 to 4 hours (LOW) • 2 to 3 hours (HIGH)

Lamb and Vegetable Stew

2 cups sliced mushrooms
1 large red bell pepper, diced
1 large carrot, cut into ½-inch-thick slices
1 small unpeeled new potato, diced
1 small parsnip, cut into ½-inch-thick slices
1 large leek, white part only, chopped
1 clove garlic, minced
½ cup reduced-sodium chicken broth
½ teaspoon dried thyme
¼ teaspoon dried rosemary
⅛ teaspoon black pepper
12 ounces lamb shoulder meat, cut into 1-inch pieces
2 tablespoons all-purpose flour
½ teaspoon salt

Slow Cooker Directions

1. Place mushrooms, bell pepper, carrot, potato, parsnip, leek and garlic in slow cooker. Add broth, thyme, rosemary and black pepper; stir. Add lamb. Cover; cook on LOW 6 to 7 hours.

2. Combine flour and 2 tablespoons liquid from slow cooker in small bowl. Stir flour mixture into slow cooker. Cover; cook 10 minutes or until thickened. Stir in salt. *Makes 4 servings*

Slow Cooker Chicken Dinner

4 boneless skinless chicken breasts
1 can (10¾ ounces) condensed cream of chicken soup, undiluted
⅓ cup milk
1 package (6 ounces) stuffing mix
1⅔ cups water

Slow Cooker Directions

Place chicken in slow cooker. Combine soup and milk in small bowl; mix well. Pour soup mixture over chicken. Combine stuffing mix and water in medium bowl. Spoon stuffing over chicken. Cover; cook on LOW 6 to 8 hours. *Makes 4 servings*

Lamb and Vegetable Stew

Layered Mexican-Style Casserole

2 cans (about 15 ounces each) hominy,* drained

1 can (about 15 ounces) black beans, rinsed and drained

1 can (about 14 ounces) diced tomatoes with garlic, basil and oregano

1 cup thick and chunky salsa

1 can (6 ounces) tomato paste

½ teaspoon ground cumin

3 (9-inch) flour tortillas

2 cups (8 ounces) shredded Monterey Jack cheese

¼ cup sliced black olives

Hominy is corn that has been treated to remove the germ and hull. It can be found with the canned vegetables or beans in most supermarkets.

Slow Cooker Directions

1. Prepare foil handles (see below). Spray slow cooker and foil handles with nonstick cooking spray.

2. Combine hominy, beans, tomatoes, salsa, tomato paste and cumin in large bowl.

3. Press one tortilla in bottom of slow cooker. (Edges of tortilla may turn up slightly.) Top with one third of hominy mixture and one third of cheese. Repeat layers. Press remaining tortilla on top. Top with remaining hominy mixture. Set aside remaining cheese.

4. Cover; cook on LOW 6 to 8 hours. Sprinkle with remaining cheese and olives. Cover; let stand 5 minutes. Pull out tortilla stack with foil handles. *Makes 6 servings*

Foil Handles: Tear off three 18×2-inch strips of heavy-duty foil or use regular foil folded to double thickness. Crisscross foil strips in spoke design and fit into slow cooker to make lifting of tortilla stack easier.

Prep Time: 15 minutes
Cook Time: 6 to 8 hours

Layered Mexican-Style Casserole

Slow Cooker Brisket of Beef

1 well-trimmed whole beef brisket (about 5 pounds)
2 teaspoons minced garlic
½ teaspoon black pepper
2 large onions, cut into ¼-inch slices and separated into rings
1 bottle (12 ounces) chili sauce
1½ cups beef broth, dark ale or water
2 tablespoons Worcestershire sauce
1 tablespoon packed brown sugar
    Red boiling potatoes, carrots, sliced parsnips or turnips (optional)

Slow Cooker Directions

1. Place brisket, fat side down, in 4- to 5-quart slow cooker. Spread garlic evenly over brisket; sprinkle with pepper. Arrange onions over brisket. Combine chili sauce, broth, Worcestershire sauce and sugar in medium bowl; pour over brisket and onions. Cover; cook on LOW 8 hours.

2. Turn brisket over; stir onions into sauce and spoon over brisket. Add vegetables, if desired. Cover; cook 1 to 2 hours or until fork-tender. Transfer brisket to cutting board. Tent with foil; let stand 10 minutes.*

3. Stir juices in slow cooker; spoon off and discard fat. (Juices may be thinned to desired consistency with water or thickened by simmering, uncovered, in saucepan.) Carve brisket across grain into thin slices. Spoon juices over brisket.   *Makes 10 to 12 servings*

At this point, brisket may be covered and refrigerated up to one day before serving. To reheat brisket, cut diagonally into thin slices. Place brisket slices and juice in large skillet. Cover and cook over medium-low heat until heated through.

Slow Cooker Brisket of Beef

Cerveza Chicken Enchilada Casserole

2 cups water

1 stalk celery, chopped

1 small carrot, chopped

1 bottle (12 ounces) Mexican beer, divided

Juice of 1 lime

1 teaspoon salt

1½ pounds boneless skinless chicken breasts

1 can (19 ounces) enchilada sauce

7 ounces white corn tortilla chips

½ medium onion, chopped

3 cups (12 ounces) shredded Cheddar cheese

Sour cream, sliced olives and cilantro (optional)

Slow Cooker Directions

1. Bring water, celery, carrot, 1 cup beer, lime juice and salt to a boil in medium saucepan over high heat. Add chicken; reduce heat to a simmer. Cook about 12 to 14 minutes or until chicken is cooked through. Remove chicken from saucepan; discard cooking liquid. Cool chicken slightly; shred.

2. Pour ½ cup enchilada sauce into slow cooker. Place tortilla chips in single layer over sauce. Cover with one third of shredded chicken. Sprinkle one third of onion over chicken. Sprinkle evenly with 1 cup cheese. Repeat twice with layers of enchilada sauce, chicken, onion and cheese. Pour remaining beer over casserole before adding last layer of cheese.

3. Cover; cook on LOW 3½ to 4 hours. Garnish with sour cream, sliced olives and cilantro, if desired.   *Makes 4 to 6 servings*

Cerveza Chicken Enchilada Casserole

Caribbean Sweet Potato & Bean Stew

2 medium sweet potatoes (about 1 pound), peeled and cut into 1-inch cubes
2 cups frozen cut green beans
1 can (about 15 ounces) **black beans,** rinsed and drained
1 can (about 14 ounces) **vegetable broth**
1 small onion, sliced
2 teaspoons Caribbean jerk seasoning
½ teaspoon dried thyme
¼ teaspoon salt
¼ teaspoon ground cinnamon
⅓ cup slivered almonds, toasted*
Hot pepper sauce (optional)

*To toast almonds, spread in single layer on baking sheet. Bake in preheated 350°F oven 8 to 10 minutes or until golden brown, stirring frequently.

Slow Cooker Directions

1. Combine sweet potatoes, beans, broth, onion, jerk seasoning, thyme, salt and cinnamon in slow cooker. Cover; cook on LOW 5 to 6 hours or until vegetables are tender.

2. Serve with almonds and hot pepper sauce, if desired.

Makes 4 servings

Prep Time: 10 minutes
Cook Time: 5 to 6 hours

Harvest Ham Supper

6 carrots, cut into 2-inch pieces
3 medium sweet potatoes, peeled and quartered
1 to 1½ pounds boneless ham
1 cup maple syrup

Slow Cooker Directions

1. Place carrots and potatoes in slow cooker. Place ham on top of vegetables. Pour syrup over ham and vegetables.

2. Cover; cook on LOW 6 to 8 hours.

Makes 6 servings

Caribbean Sweet Potato & Bean Stew

South-of-the-Border Cumin Chicken

1 package (16 ounces) frozen bell pepper stir-fry mixture, thawed *or* 3 bell peppers, thinly sliced*

4 chicken drumsticks, skin removed

4 chicken thighs, skin removed

1 can (about 14 ounces) stewed tomatoes

1 tablespoon hot pepper sauce

2 teaspoons sugar

1¾ teaspoons ground cumin, divided

1¼ teaspoons salt

1 teaspoon dried oregano

¼ cup chopped fresh cilantro

1 to 2 limes, cut into wedges

Hot cooked rice or corn tortilla chips (optional)

*If using fresh bell peppers, add 1 small onion, chopped.

Slow Cooker Directions

1. Place bell pepper mixture in slow cooker; arrange chicken on top of peppers.

2. Combine tomatoes, hot pepper sauce, sugar, 1 teaspoon cumin, salt and oregano in large bowl. Pour over chicken mixture. Cover; cook on LOW 8 hours or on HIGH 4 hours or until meat is just beginning to fall off bone.

3. Place chicken in shallow serving bowl. Stir remaining ¾ teaspoon cumin into tomato mixture; pour over chicken. Sprinkle with cilantro. Serve with lime wedges, cooked rice or tortilla chips, if desired.

Makes 4 servings

note

Cumin is an ancient spice that dates back to the Old Testament. It is available in both seed and ground forms. The flavor is nutty and earthy. Cumin is very popular in Middle-Eastern, Asian and Latin American cuisine.

South-of-the-Border Cumin Chicken

Turkey and Macaroni

1 teaspoon vegetable oil

1½ pounds ground turkey

2 cans (10¾ ounces each) condensed tomato soup, undiluted

1 can (16 ounces) corn, drained

½ cup chopped onion

1 can (4 ounces) sliced mushrooms, drained

2 tablespoons ketchup

1 tablespoon mustard

Salt and black pepper

2 cups uncooked macaroni, cooked and drained

Slow Cooker Directions

1. Heat oil in large nonstick skillet over medium-high heat. Brown turkey, stirring to break up meat. Transfer turkey to slow cooker.

2. Add soup, corn, onion, mushrooms, ketchup, mustard, salt and pepper to slow cooker; mix well. Cover; cook on LOW 6 to 8 hours or on HIGH 3 to 4 hours. Stir in macaroni. Cover; cook on LOW 30 minutes.   *Makes 4 to 6 servings*

Broccoli & Cheese Strata

2 cups chopped broccoli florets

4 slices firm white bread, ½ inch thick

4 teaspoons butter

1½ cups (6 ounces) shredded Cheddar cheese

1½ cups milk

3 eggs

½ teaspoon salt

½ teaspoon hot pepper sauce

⅛ teaspoon black pepper

Slow Cooker Directions

1. Cook broccoli in boiling water 10 minutes or until tender. Drain. Spread 1 side of each bread slice with 1 teaspoon butter. Arrange 2 slices bread, buttered side up, in greased 1-quart casserole that will fit in slow cooker. Top with cheese, broccoli and remaining 2 bread slices, buttered side down.

2. Beat milk, eggs, salt, hot pepper sauce and black pepper in medium bowl. Pour over bread.

3. Place small wire rack in 5-quart slow cooker. Pour in 1 cup water. Place casserole on rack. Cover; cook on HIGH 3 hours.

Makes 4 servings

Chili Verde

¾ pound boneless lean pork, cut into 1-inch cubes

1 can (about 15 ounces) Great Northern beans, rinsed and drained

1 can (about 14 ounces) chicken broth

1 pound fresh tomatillos, husks removed, rinsed and coarsely chopped

1 large onion, halved and thinly sliced

1 can (4 ounces) diced mild green chiles

6 cloves garlic, chopped or sliced

1 teaspoon ground cumin

Salt and black pepper

½ cup lightly packed fresh cilantro, chopped

Sour cream

Slow Cooker Directions

1. Spray large skillet with nonstick cooking spray; heat over medium-high heat. Add pork; cook until browned on all sides.

2. Combine pork and all remaining ingredients except cilantro and sour cream in slow cooker. Cover; cook on HIGH 3 to 4 hours.

3. Season to taste with salt and pepper. Shred pork in slow cooker. Reduce heat to LOW. Stir in cilantro; cover and cook 10 minutes. Serve with sour cream.

Makes 4 servings

Slow Cooker Seafood Bouillabaisse

1 medium onion, chopped
½ bulb fennel, chopped
2 cloves garlic, minced
1 can (28 ounces) tomato purée
2 bottles (12 ounces each) beer, divided
8 ounces clam juice
1 bay leaf
½ teaspoon salt
¼ teaspoon black pepper
2 cups water
½ pound red snapper, pin bones removed and cut into 1-inch pieces
8 mussels, scrubbed and debearded
8 cherry stone clams
8 large raw shrimp, unpeeled
4 lemon wedges
Italian parsley sprigs (optional)

Slow Cooker Directions

1. Combine onion, fennel and garlic in large skillet; cook and stir over medium-high heat until onion is soft and translucent. Transfer mixture to 5-quart slow cooker. Pour tomato purée, 1 bottle of beer, clam juice, bay leaf, salt and pepper into slow cooker. Cover; cook on LOW 6 to 8 hours or on HIGH 3 to 4 hours.

2. During last 30 minutes of cooking, pour remaining bottle of beer into large stockpot. Add water. Place steamer insert in stockpot (do not allow water to touch the insert). Bring to a boil. Place red snapper, mussels, clams and shrimp into insert. Cover and steam 4 to 8 minutes, discarding any mussels or clams that do not open.

3. Remove and discard bay leaf. Ladle broth into soup bowls. Place fish and shellfish on top. Serve with lemon wedges. Garnish with parsley sprigs. *Makes 4 servings*

Slow Cooker Seafood Bouillabaisse

Chipotle Cornish Hens

3 small carrots, cut into ½-inch rounds
3 stalks celery, cut into ½-inch pieces
1 onion, chopped
1 can (7 ounces) chipotle peppers in adobo sauce, divided
2 cups prepared cornbread stuffing
4 Cornish hens (about 1½ pounds each)
  Salt and black pepper
  Fresh parsley, chopped (optional)

Slow Cooker Directions

1. Coat 5- to 6-quart slow cooker with nonstick cooking spray. Add carrots, celery and onion.

2. Pour chipotles into small bowl. Finely chop ½ chipotle pepper and mix into prepared stuffing. Remove remaining peppers from adobo sauce and reserve for another use. Finely chop remaining ½ chipotle pepper and add to adobo sauce.*

3. Rinse and dry hens, removing giblets, if any. Season inside and outside of hens with salt and pepper. Fill each hen with about ½ cup stuffing. Rub adobo sauce onto hens. Place hens in slow cooker with necks down and legs up. Cover; cook on HIGH 3½ to 4 hours or until cooked through (165°F).

4. Transfer hens to serving platter. Remove vegetables with slotted spoon and arrange around hens. Garnish with parsley. Spoon cooking juices over hens and vegetables, if desired.

Makes 4 servings

*For spicier flavor, use 1 chipotle pepper in stuffing and 1 chipotle pepper in sauce.

Prep Time: 15 minutes
Cook Time: 3½ to 4 hours

Chipotle Cornish Hens

Chicken and Wild Rice Casserole

3 tablespoons olive oil

2 slices bacon, chopped

1½ pounds chicken thighs, trimmed of excess skin

½ cup diced onion

½ cup diced celery

2 tablespoons Worcestershire sauce

¾ teaspoon salt

½ teaspoon dried sage

¼ teaspoon black pepper

1 cup uncooked converted long grain white rice

1 package (4 ounces) wild rice

6 ounces cremini mushrooms,* quartered

3 cups hot chicken broth (or enough to cover chicken)

Additional salt and black pepper (optional)

2 tablespoons chopped fresh parsley

Substitute white button mushrooms if cremini mushrooms are not available.

Slow Cooker Directions

1. Evenly coat bottom of slow cooker with oil. Microwave bacon on HIGH 1 minute. Transfer to slow cooker. Place chicken in slow cooker, skin side down. Add remaining ingredients in order given, except parsley. Cover; cook on LOW 3 to 4 hours or until rice is tender.

2. Remove cover; let stand 15 minutes. Add additional salt and pepper, if desired. Remove skin before serving, if desired. Garnish with parsley.   *Makes 4 to 6 servings*

Prep Time: 15 minutes
Cook Time: 3 to 4 hours

Chicken and Wild Rice Casserole

Caribbean Shrimp with Rice

- 1 package (12 ounces) frozen shrimp, thawed
- ½ cup reduced-sodium chicken broth
- 1 clove garlic, minced
- 1 teaspoon chili powder
- ½ teaspoon salt
- ½ teaspoon dried oregano
- 1 cup frozen peas, thawed
- ½ cup diced tomatoes
- 2 cups cooked long grain white rice

Slow Cooker Directions

1. Combine shrimp, broth, garlic, chili powder, salt and oregano in slow cooker. Cover; cook on LOW 2 hours.

2. Add peas and tomatoes. Cover; cook on LOW 15 minutes.

3. Stir in rice. Cover; cook on LOW an additional 15 minutes.

Makes 4 servings

Prep Time: 10 minutes
Cook Time: 2½ hours

Easy Beef Stew

- 1½ to 2 pounds beef stew meat
- 4 medium potatoes, cubed
- 4 carrots, cut into 1½-inch pieces *or* 4 cups baby carrots
- 1 medium onion, cut into 8 pieces
- 2 cans (8 ounces each) tomato sauce
- 1 teaspoon salt
- ½ teaspoon black pepper

Slow Cooker Directions

Combine all ingredients in slow cooker. Cover; cook on LOW 8 to 10 hours or until vegetables are tender. *Makes 6 to 8 servings*

Caribbean Shrimp with Rice

Chicken Pilaf

2 pounds chopped cooked chicken
2½ cups water
2 cans (8 ounces each) tomato sauce
1⅓ cups uncooked converted long grain rice
1 cup chopped onion
1 cup chopped celery
1 cup chopped green bell pepper
⅔ cup sliced black olives
¼ cup sliced almonds
¼ cup (½ stick) butter, cubed
2 cloves garlic, minced
2½ teaspoons salt
½ teaspoon ground allspice
½ teaspoon ground turmeric
¼ teaspoon curry powder
¼ teaspoon black pepper

Slow Cooker Directions

Combine all ingredients in slow cooker; stir well. Cover; cook on LOW 6 to 8 hours or on HIGH 3 to 4 hours.   *Makes 10 servings*

Weeknight Chili

1 pound ground beef or ground turkey
1 package (1¼ ounces) chili seasoning mix
1 can (about 14 ounces) diced tomatoes with green chiles
1 can (about 15 ounces) red kidney beans, rinsed and drained
1 can (8 ounces) tomato sauce
1 cup (4 ounces) shredded Cheddar cheese

Slow Cooker Directions

1. Brown beef in large skillet over medium-high heat 6 to 8 minutes, stirring to break up meat. Drain fat. Stir in seasoning mix.

2. Place beef, tomatoes, beans and tomato sauce in slow cooker. Cover; cook on LOW 4 to 6 hours. Top each serving with cheese.
Makes 4 servings

Chicken Pilaf

Squash and Beef Slow Cooker Stew

1 tablespoon vegetable oil

1 medium yellow onion, finely chopped

1 clove garlic, minced

2 cans (about 14 ounces each) diced tomatoes

1 small butternut or buttercup squash, cut into 1-inch cubes (2 cups)

1 pound beef stew meat, cut into bite-size chunks

1 can (about 15 ounces) butter beans, rinsed and drained

½ cup beef broth

1 teaspoon canned or fresh minced jalapeño pepper

½ teaspoon chili powder

½ teaspoon dried oregano

½ teaspoon salt

¼ teaspoon ground cumin

¼ teaspoon black pepper

Slow Cooker Directions

1. Heat oil in medium skillet over medium heat. Add onion and garlic; cook and stir 5 to 8 minutes or until onion is golden brown. (Do not let garlic burn.) Spoon onion and garlic into 5-quart slow cooker.

2. Add tomatoes, squash, beef, beans, broth, jalapeño pepper, chili powder, oregano, salt, cumin and black pepper to slow cooker.

3. Cover; cook on HIGH 5 to 7 hours. Turn off heat; remove cover. Let stand 30 minutes to thicken. *Makes 4 to 6 servings*

Note: To save time, skip Step 1. Place raw onion and garlic in slow cooker. Add remaining ingredients and proceed as directed above.

Squash and Beef Slow Cooker Stew

Jerk Pork and Sweet Potato Stew

 2 tablespoons all-purpose flour

¼ teaspoon salt

¼ teaspoon black pepper

1¼ pounds pork shoulder, cut into bite-size pieces

 2 tablespoons vegetable oil

 1 large sweet potato, peeled and diced

 1 cup thawed frozen or canned corn

¼ cup minced green onions, green part only, divided

½ medium scotch bonnet chile or jalapeño pepper,* seeded and
  minced

 1 clove garlic, minced

⅛ teaspoon ground allspice

 1 cup chicken broth

 1 tablespoon lime juice

 2 cups hot cooked rice (optional)

Chile peppers can sting and irritate the skin, so wear rubber gloves when handling and do not touch your eyes.

Slow Cooker Directions

1. Combine flour, salt and black pepper in resealable food storage bag. Add pork and shake well to coat. Heat oil in large skillet over medium heat. Add pork in single layer (cook in 2 batches, if necessary); brown on both sides, about 5 minutes. Transfer to slow cooker.

2. Add sweet potato, corn, 2 tablespoons green onions, chile, garlic and allspice. Stir in broth. Cover; cook on LOW 5 to 6 hours.

3. Stir in lime juice and remaining 2 tablespoons green onions. Serve stew over rice, if desired.   *Makes 4 servings*

Prep Time: 15 minutes
Cook Time: 5 to 6 hours

Jerk Pork and Sweet Potato Stew

classic casserole favorites

It's a Keeper Casserole

  1 tablespoon vegetable oil
  ½ cup chopped onion
  ¼ cup chopped green bell pepper
  1 clove garlic, minced
  2 tablespoons all-purpose flour
  1 teaspoon sugar
  ½ teaspoon salt
  ½ teaspoon dried basil
  ½ teaspoon black pepper
  1 package (about 16 ounces) frozen meatballs, cooked
  1 can (about 14 ounces) whole tomatoes, cut up and drained
1½ cups cooked vegetables (any combination)
  1 teaspoon beef bouillon granules
  1 teaspoon Worcestershire sauce
  1 can refrigerated buttermilk biscuit dough (8 count)

1. Preheat oven to 400°F. Heat oil in large saucepan over medium heat. Cook and stir onion, bell pepper and garlic 5 minutes or until vegetables are tender.

2. Stir in flour, sugar, salt, basil and black pepper. Slowly stir in meatballs, tomatoes, vegetables, bouillon and Worcestershire sauce. Cook and stir until slightly thickened and bubbling; pour into 2-quart casserole.

3. Unroll biscuits; place on top of casserole. Bake, uncovered, 15 minutes or until biscuits are golden. *Makes 4 servings*

Ham, Poblano and Potato Casserole

¼ **cup (½ stick) butter**

¼ **cup all-purpose flour**

1½ **cups whole milk**

2 **pounds baking potatoes, thinly sliced and cut into bite-size pieces**

6 **ounces thinly sliced ham, cut into bite-size pieces**

1 **poblano pepper, cut into thin strips (about 1 cup)**

1 **cup corn**

1 **cup chopped red bell pepper**

1 **cup finely chopped onion**

1½ **teaspoons salt**

¼ **teaspoon black pepper**

¼ **teaspoon ground nutmeg**

1½ **cups (6 ounces) shredded sharp Cheddar cheese**

1. Preheat oven to 350°F. Spray 13×9-inch baking dish with nonstick cooking spray; set aside.

2. Melt butter in medium saucepan over medium heat. Add flour; whisk until smooth. Add milk; whisk until smooth. Cook and stir 5 to 7 minutes or until thickened. Remove from heat; set aside.

3. Layer one third of potatoes, half of ham, half of poblano pepper, half of corn, half of bell pepper and half of onion in prepared baking dish. Sprinkle with half of salt, pepper and nutmeg. Repeat layers. Top with remaining third of potatoes. Spoon white sauce evenly over top.

4. Cover with foil; bake 45 minutes. Uncover; bake 30 minutes more or until potatoes are tender. Sprinkle with cheese; bake 5 minutes or until cheese is melted. Let stand 15 minutes before serving.

Makes 6 servings

Tip: Use a food processor with the slicing blade attachment to thinly slice potatoes.

Ham, Poblano and Potato Casserole

Chili-Chicken Enchiladas

Nonstick cooking spray

3 cups (12 ounces) shredded Cheddar and/or Monterey Jack cheese, divided

1½ cups sour cream, divided

¾ cup roasted red peppers, drained, chopped and divided

1 can (7 ounces) ORTEGA® Diced Green Chiles, divided

2 cups diced cooked chicken

1 can (10 ounces) ORTEGA® Enchilada Sauce

8 (8-inch) ORTEGA® Soft Flour Tortillas

Preheat oven to 350°F. Spray 13×9-inch glass baking dish with cooking spray.

Reserve 1½ cups cheese, ½ cup sour cream and ¼ cup each red peppers and green chiles; set aside.

Mix chicken with remaining cheese, sour cream, red peppers and green chiles in medium bowl.

Spread about 2 teaspoons enchilada sauce over each tortilla. Top each with about ½ cup chicken mixture. Roll up tortillas; arrange, seam side down, in baking dish.

Top tortillas with remaining enchilada sauce. Sprinkle with the reserved cheese.

Cover with foil. Bake for 50 to 60 minutes or until hot, removing foil during last 5 minutes of baking time.

Spoon reserved sour cream over top and sprinkle with the reserved red peppers and green chiles.

Makes 4 servings (2 enchiladas each)

Tip: Rotisserie chicken is a great time-saver for busy cooks. Try using it for the diced cooked chicken in this recipe.

Chili-Chicken Enchiladas

Southwestern Corn and Pasta Casserole

  2 tablespoons vegetable oil
  1 large red bell pepper, chopped
  1 small onion, chopped
  1 small jalapeño pepper,* minced
  1 clove garlic, minced
  1 cup sliced mushrooms
  2 cups frozen corn
½ teaspoon salt
¼ teaspoon ground cumin
¼ teaspoon chili powder
  4 ounces whole wheat elbow macaroni, cooked
1½ cups milk
  1 tablespoon butter
  1 tablespoon all-purpose flour
  1 cup (4 ounces) shredded pepper jack cheese
  1 slice whole wheat bread, cut or torn into ½-inch pieces

Jalapeño peppers can sting and irritate the skin, so wear rubber gloves when handling peppers and do not touch your eyes.

1. Preheat oven to 350°F. Grease 3-quart baking dish; set aside.

2. Heat oil in large skillet. Add bell pepper, onion, jalapeño and garlic. Cook and stir over medium-high heat 5 minutes. Add mushrooms; cook 5 minutes. Add corn, salt, cumin and chili powder. Reduce heat to low; simmer 5 minutes or until corn thaws. Stir in macaroni; set aside.

3. Bring milk to a simmer in small saucepan. Melt butter in large saucepan; stir in flour until smooth. Gradually stir in hot milk. Cook and stir over medium-low heat until slightly thickened. Gradually stir in cheese; cook and stir over very low heat until cheese melts. Stir macaroni mixture into cheese sauce; mix well.

4. Spoon into prepared baking dish. Sprinkle bread pieces over casserole. Bake 20 to 25 minutes or until bubbly. Let stand 5 minutes before serving. *Makes 4 servings*

Southwestern Corn and Pasta Casserole

Pizza Casserole

 2 cups uncooked rotini or other spiral pasta
1½ to 2 pounds ground beef
 1 medium onion, chopped
   Salt and black pepper
 1 can (about 15 ounces) pizza sauce
 1 can (8 ounces) tomato sauce
 1 can (6 ounces) tomato paste
 ½ teaspoon sugar
 ½ teaspoon garlic salt
 ½ teaspoon dried oregano
 2 cups (8 ounces) shredded mozzarella cheese
12 to 15 slices pepperoni

1. Preheat oven to 350°F. Cook pasta according to package directions; drain and set aside.

2. Meanwhile, cook and stir ground beef and onion in large skillet over medium-high heat 6 to 8 minutes, stirring to break up meat. Drain fat. Season with salt and pepper.

3. Combine pasta, pizza sauce, tomato sauce, tomato paste, sugar, garlic salt and oregano in large bowl. Add beef mixture; stir until blended.

4. Place half of mixture in 3-quart casserole; top with 1 cup cheese. Repeat layers. Arrange pepperoni slices on top.

5. Bake 25 to 30 minutes or until heated through and cheese is melted. *Makes 6 servings*

Pizza Casserole

Ham Asparagus Gratin

   1 can (10¾ ounces) Campbell's® Condensed Cream of
       Asparagus Soup
   ½ cup milk
   ¼ teaspoon onion powder
   ⅛ teaspoon black pepper
   1½ cups cooked cut asparagus
   1½ cups cubed cooked ham
   2¼ cups corkscrew-shaped pasta (rotini), cooked and drained
   1 cup shredded Cheddar *or* Swiss cheese

1. Stir the soup, milk, onion powder, black pepper, asparagus, ham, pasta and ½ **cup** of the cheese in a 12×8×2-inch shallow baking pan.

2. Bake at 400°F. for 25 minutes or until hot. Stir.

3. Sprinkle with the remaining cheese. Bake 5 minutes more or until cheese melts.   *Makes 4 servings*

Substitution: Substitute 1½ cups cooked cubed chicken for cubed cooked ham.

Prep Time: 20 minutes
Cook Time: 30 minutes

Tuscan Pot Pie

   ¾ pound sweet or hot Italian sausage
   1 jar (26 to 28 ounces) chunky vegetable or mushroom pasta sauce
   1 can (about 15 ounces) cannellini beans, rinsed and drained
   ½ teaspoon dried thyme
   1½ cups (6 ounces) shredded mozzarella cheese
   1 package (8 ounces) refrigerated crescent roll dough

1. Preheat oven to 425°F. Remove sausage from casings. Brown sausage in medium ovenproof skillet over medium-high heat, stirring to break up meat. Drain fat.

continued on page 136

Ham Asparagus Gratin

Tuscan Pot Pie, continued

2. Add pasta sauce, beans and thyme to skillet. Simmer uncovered over medium heat 5 minutes. Remove from heat; stir in cheese.

3. Unroll crescent dough; divide into triangles. Arrange in spiral with points of dough toward center, covering sausage mixture completely. Bake 12 minutes or until crust is golden brown and meat mixture is bubbly. *Makes 4 to 6 servings*

Note: To remove a sausage casing, use a paring knife to slit the casing at one end. Be careful not to cut through the sausage. Grasp the cut edge and gently pull the casing away from the sausage.

Prep and Cook Time: 27 minutes

Southwest Spaghetti Squash

1 spaghetti squash (about 3 pounds)
1 can (about 14 ounces) Mexican-style diced tomatoes, undrained
1 can (about 15 ounces) black beans, rinsed and drained
¾ cup (3 ounces) shredded Monterey Jack cheese, divided
¼ cup finely chopped cilantro
1 teaspoon ground cumin
¼ teaspoon garlic salt
¼ teaspoon black pepper

1. Preheat oven to 350°F. Spray baking pan and 1½-quart baking dish with nonstick cooking spray. Cut squash in half lengthwise. Remove and discard seeds. Place squash, cut side down, in prepared baking pan. Bake 45 minutes to 1 hour or just until tender. Shred hot squash with fork; place in large bowl. (Use oven mitts to protect hands.)

2. Add tomatoes, beans, ½ cup cheese, cilantro, cumin, garlic salt and pepper to squash; toss well. Spoon mixture into prepared dish. Sprinkle with remaining ¼ cup cheese.

3. Bake, uncovered, 30 to 35 minutes or until heated through. Serve immediately. *Makes 4 servings*

Southwest Spaghetti Squash

Easy Lamb Pie

- 1 pound ground AMERICAN LAMB
- 2 cups light sour cream
- 2 cans (10¾ ounces each) mushroom soup with roasted garlic
- 2 teaspoons Italian seasoning
- 2 teaspoons garlic salt
- 2 teaspoons ground black pepper
- 8 ounces (1⅔ cups) frozen peas and carrots, defrosted
- 1 sheet frozen puff pastry, unfolded and defrosted
  Butter cooking spray

Spray a medium skillet with nonstick cooking spray. Add lamb and cook over medium-high heat until brown, stirring to crumble. Drain well.

In large bowl, combine sour cream, undiluted soup, Italian seasoning, garlic salt and pepper. Stir in cooked lamb, peas and carrots.

Spray a 9×9-inch baking dish with nonstick cooking spray. Pour in lamb mixture, spreading evenly. Top with pastry, turning under edges to fit pan. Using a sharp knife, make slits in pastry. Spray with butter cooking spray. Bake in 425°F oven for 20 minutes or until pastry is golden brown and filling is bubbling. Let stand for 5 minutes.

Makes 8 servings

Prep Time: 5 minutes
Cook Time: 20 minutes

Favorite Recipe from **American Lamb Board**

E-Z Chicken Tortilla Bake

- 1 can (10.75 ounces) condensed tomato soup, undiluted
- 1 cup ORTEGA® Thick & Chunky Salsa
- ½ cup milk
- 2 cups cubed cooked chicken
- 8 (8-inch) ORTEGA® Soft Flour Tortillas, cut into 1-inch pieces
- 1 cup (4 ounces) shredded Cheddar cheese, divided

Preheat oven to 400°F. Mix soup, salsa, milk, chicken, tortillas and ½ cup cheese in 2-quart shallow baking dish. Cover; bake 30 minutes or until hot. Top with remaining ½ cup cheese.

Makes 4 servings

Tip: Use turkey instead of chicken for an E–Z Turkey Tortilla Bake.

Note: Two whole chicken breasts (about 10 ounces each) will yield about 2 cups of chopped cooked chicken.

Prep Time: 10 minutes
Start to Finish: 40 minutes

Smoked Sausage and Sauerkraut Casserole

6 fully cooked smoked sausage links, such as German or Polish sausage (about 1½ pounds)

⅓ cup water

¼ cup packed brown sugar

2 tablespoons country-style Dijon mustard, Dijon mustard or German-style mustard

1 teaspoon caraway seeds

½ teaspoon dried dill weed

1 jar (32 ounces) sauerkraut, drained

1 small green bell pepper, diced

½ cup (2 ounces) shredded Swiss cheese

1. Place sausage and water in large skillet. Cover; bring to a boil over medium heat. Reduce heat to low; simmer, covered, 10 minutes. Uncover; simmer until water evaporates and sausage is lightly browned.

2. Meanwhile, combine sugar, mustard, caraway seeds and dill in medium saucepan; stir until blended. Add sauerkraut and bell pepper; stir until well blended. Cook, covered, over medium heat 10 minutes or until very hot.

3. Spoon sauerkraut mixture into microwavable 2- to 3-quart casserole. Place sausage on sauerkraut; sprinkle with cheese. Cover; microwave on HIGH 30 seconds or until cheese melts.

Makes 6 servings

No-Chop Pastitsio

    1 pound 90% lean ground beef or ground lamb
 1½ cups mild picante sauce
    1 can (8 ounces) tomato sauce
    1 tablespoon sugar
 ½ teaspoon ground allspice
 ½ teaspoon ground cinnamon
 ¼ teaspoon ground nutmeg, divided
    8 ounces uncooked elbow macaroni
    3 tablespoons butter
    3 tablespoons all-purpose flour
 1½ cups milk
 ½ teaspoon salt
 ¼ teaspoon black pepper
    2 eggs, beaten
 ½ cup grated Parmesan cheese

1. Preheat oven to 350°F. Lightly coat 9-inch square baking dish with nonstick cooking spray; set aside.

2. Brown beef in large skillet over medium-high heat 6 to 8 minutes, stirring to break up meat. Drain fat. Add picante sauce, tomato sauce, sugar, allspice, cinnamon and ⅛ teaspoon nutmeg; bring to a boil. Reduce heat; simmer, uncovered, 10 minutes, stirring frequently.

3. Meanwhile, cook macaroni according to package directions; drain. Place in prepared baking dish.

4. Melt butter in medium saucepan over medium heat. Add flour; mix until smooth. Add milk; cook and stir until thickened. Remove from heat. Add about ½ cup white sauce mixture to eggs in small bowl; whisk well. Add egg mixture to remaining white sauce in saucepan. Stir in cheese.

5. Mix about ½ cup white sauce into macaroni; toss to coat completely. Spread meat sauce over macaroni. Top with remaining white sauce. Sprinkle evenly with remaining ⅛ teaspoon nutmeg.

6. Bake, uncovered, 30 to 40 minutes or until knife inserted into center comes out clean. Let stand 15 to 20 minutes before serving.

Makes 6 servings

No-Chop Pastitsio

Pork and Corn Bread Stuffing Casserole

- ½ **teaspoon paprika**
- ¼ **teaspoon salt**
- ¼ **teaspoon black pepper**
- ¼ **teaspoon garlic powder**
- 4 **bone-in pork chops (about 1¾ pounds)**
- 2 **tablespoons butter**
- 1½ **cups chopped onions**
- ¾ **cup thinly sliced celery**
- ¾ **cup matchstick-size carrots***
- ¼ **cup chopped fresh parsley**
- 1 **can (about 14 ounces) chicken broth**
- 4 **cups corn bread stuffing**

*Matchstick carrots are sometimes called shredded carrots, and are sold with other prepared vegetables in the supermarket produce section.

1. Preheat oven to 350°F. Lightly coat 13×9-inch baking dish with nonstick cooking spray; set aside.

2. Combine paprika, salt, pepper and garlic powder in small bowl. Season both sides of pork chops with paprika mixture.

3. Melt butter in large skillet over medium-high heat. Add pork chops. Cook 2 minutes or just until browned. Flip; cook 1 minute longer. Transfer to plate; set aside.

4. Add onions, celery, carrots and parsley to skillet. Cook and stir 4 minutes or until onions are translucent. Add broth; bring to a boil over high heat. Remove from heat; add stuffing and fluff with fork. Transfer mixture to prepared baking dish. Place browned pork chops on top. Cover; bake 25 minutes or until pork is barely pink in center. *Makes 4 servings*

Variation: For a one-skillet meal, use an ovenproof skillet. Place browned pork chops on mixture in skillet; cover and bake as directed.

Pork and Corn Bread Stuffing Casserole

Tamale Pie

   1 tablespoon vegetable oil
   ½ cup chopped onion
   ⅓ cup chopped red bell pepper
   1 clove garlic, minced
   ¾ pound ground turkey
   ¾ teaspoon chili powder
   ½ teaspoon dried oregano
   1 can (about 14 ounces) Mexican-style stewed tomatoes
   1 can (about 15 ounces) chili beans in mild chili sauce, undrained
   1 cup corn
   ¼ teaspoon black pepper
   1 package (8½ ounces) corn muffin mix plus ingredients to
       prepare mix
   2 cups (8 ounces) taco cheese blend, divided

1. Preheat oven to 375°F. Lightly grease 1½- to 2-quart casserole; set aside.

2. Heat oil in large skillet over medium heat. Add onion and bell pepper; cook until crisp-tender. Stir in garlic. Add turkey; cook and stir until turkey is no longer pink. Stir in chili powder and oregano. Add tomatoes; cook and stir 2 minutes. Stir in beans, corn and black pepper; simmer 10 minutes or until liquid is reduced by about half.

3. Prepare corn muffin mix according to package directions; stir in ½ cup cheese.

4. Spread half of turkey mixture in prepared casserole; sprinkle with ¾ cup cheese. Repeat layers. Spread corn muffin batter over top. Bake 20 to 22 minutes or until light golden brown.

Makes 4 to 6 servings

Tamale Pie

Baked Black Bean Chili

1½ pounds 90% lean ground beef
¼ cup chopped onion
¼ cup chopped green bell pepper
1 can (about 15 ounces) black beans, rinsed and drained
1 can (about 14 ounces) diced tomatoes with green chiles
1 can (about 14 ounces) beef broth
1 can (8 ounces) tomato sauce
¼ cup plus 1 tablespoon chili powder
1 tablespoon sugar
1 tablespoon ground cumin
1 teaspoon dried minced onion
⅛ teaspoon garlic powder
⅛ teaspoon ground ginger
1½ cups (6 ounces) shredded Mexican cheese blend

1. Preheat oven to 350°F. Cook beef, onion and bell pepper in large skillet over medium-high heat 6 to 8 minutes, stirring to break up meat. Drain fat. Transfer to 4-quart casserole.

2. Add remaining ingredients except cheese; stir until well blended. Cover; bake 30 minutes, stirring every 10 minutes. Top each serving with cheese.   *Makes 6 to 8 servings*

note

Chili powder varies from brand to brand. It is usually a combination of dried chiles, garlic, salt, oregano, cumin, coriander and cloves.

Baked Black Bean Chili

Sausage Pizza Pie Casserole

8 ounces mild Italian sausage, casings removed
1 package (13.8 ounces) refrigerated pizza dough
½ cup tomato sauce
2 tablespoons chopped fresh basil *or* 2 teaspoons dried basil
½ teaspoon dried oregano
¼ teaspoon red pepper flakes
3 ounces whole mushrooms, quartered
½ cup thinly sliced red onion
½ cup thinly sliced green bell pepper
½ cup seeded diced tomato
½ cup sliced pitted black olives
8 slices smoked provolone cheese
2 tablespoons grated Parmesan and Romano cheese blend

1. Preheat oven to 350°F. Lightly coat 13×9-inch baking dish with nonstick cooking spray; set aside.

2. Heat large skillet over medium-high heat. Add sausage; cook until browned, stirring frequently to break up meat. Drain fat.

3. Line prepared dish with pizza dough. Spoon tomato sauce evenly over dough; sprinkle with basil, oregano and pepper flakes. Layer with sausage, mushrooms, onion, bell pepper, tomato, olives and provolone cheese. Roll down sides of crust to form a rim.

4. Bake 20 to 25 minutes or until crust is golden brown. Sprinkle with cheese blend; let stand 5 minutes before serving.

Makes 4 to 6 servings

Sausage Pizza Pie Casserole

Split-Biscuit Chicken Pie

1 package (6 ounces) refrigerated biscuit dough
⅓ cup butter
⅓ cup all-purpose flour
2½ cups whole milk
1 tablespoon chicken bouillon granules
½ teaspoon dried thyme
½ teaspoon black pepper
4 cups diced cooked chicken
2 jars (4 ounces each) diced pimientos
1 cup frozen peas, thawed

1. Bake biscuits according to package directions; set aside.

2. Preheat oven to 350°F. Lightly coat 12×8-inch baking dish or 2-quart casserole with nonstick cooking spray; set aside.

3. Melt butter in large skillet over medium heat. Add flour; whisk until smooth. Add milk, bouillon, thyme and pepper; whisk until smooth. Cook and stir until thickened. Remove from heat. Stir in chicken, pimientos and peas. Pour mixture into prepared baking dish. Bake 30 minutes.

4. Split biscuits in half; arrange cut side down on top of chicken mixture. Bake 3 minutes or until biscuits are heated through.

Makes 4 to 5 servings

Split-Biscuit Chicken Pie

Tuna Noodle Casserole

     Nonstick cooking spray
  8 ounces wide whole wheat egg noodles
  ½ cup finely chopped onion
  1 can (10 ounces) condensed cream of mushroom soup, undiluted
  ½ cup sour cream
  ½ cup milk
  ⅛ teaspoon ground red pepper
  12 ounces white tuna packed in water, drained and broken into chunks
  1½ cups frozen peas
  1 slice whole wheat or multigrain bread
  ½ teaspoon paprika

1. Preheat oven to 350°F. Spray 2½-quart casserole with cooking spray; set aside. Cook noodles according to package directions. Drain; return to saucepan.

2. Meanwhile, coat large skillet with cooking spray. Add onion; cook over medium heat 4 to 5 minutes or until tender. Stir in soup, sour cream, milk and red pepper until well blended. Remove from heat. Add soup mixture, tuna and peas to noodles. Toss well; transfer mixture to prepared casserole.

3. Tear bread into pieces; place in food processor. Process until finely minced. Sprinkle evenly over casserole; top with paprika. Spray top of casserole with cooking spray. Bake 30 to 35 minutes or until heated through.   *Makes 6 servings*

The publisher would like to thank the companies listed below for the use of their recipes in this publication.

American Lamb Board

Bob Evans®

California Olive Industry

Campbell Soup Company

Cream of Wheat® Cereal

The Hershey Company

Jennie-O Turkey Store, LLC

Ortega®, A Division of B&G Foods, Inc.

Riviana Foods Inc.

Veg•All®

conversion chart

VOLUME MEASUREMENTS (dry)

$^1/_8$ teaspoon = 0.5 mL
$^1/_4$ teaspoon = 1 mL
$^1/_2$ teaspoon = 2 mL
$^3/_4$ teaspoon = 4 mL
1 teaspoon = 5 mL
1 tablespoon = 15 mL
2 tablespoons = 30 mL
$^1/_4$ cup = 60 mL
$^1/_3$ cup = 75 mL
$^1/_2$ cup = 125 mL
$^2/_3$ cup = 150 mL
$^3/_4$ cup = 175 mL
1 cup = 250 mL
2 cups = 1 pint = 500 mL
3 cups = 750 mL
4 cups = 1 quart = 1 L

VOLUME MEASUREMENTS (fluid)

1 fluid ounce (2 tablespoons) = 30 mL
4 fluid ounces ($^1/_2$ cup) = 125 mL
8 fluid ounces (1 cup) = 250 mL
12 fluid ounces (1$^1/_2$ cups) = 375 mL
16 fluid ounces (2 cups) = 500 mL

WEIGHTS (mass)

$^1/_2$ ounce = 15 g
1 ounce = 30 g
3 ounces = 90 g
4 ounces = 120 g
8 ounces = 225 g
10 ounces = 285 g
12 ounces = 360 g
16 ounces = 1 pound = 450 g

DIMENSIONS

$^1/_{16}$ inch = 2 mm
$^1/_8$ inch = 3 mm
$^1/_4$ inch = 6 mm
$^1/_2$ inch = 1.5 cm
$^3/_4$ inch = 2 cm
1 inch = 2.5 cm

OVEN TEMPERATURES

250°F = 120°C
275°F = 140°C
300°F = 150°C
325°F = 160°C
350°F = 180°C
375°F = 190°C
400°F = 200°C
425°F = 220°C
450°F = 230°C

BAKING PAN SIZES

Utensil	Size in Inches/Quarts	Metric Volume	Size in Centimeters
Baking or Cake Pan (square or rectangular)	8×8×2	2 L	20×20×5
	9×9×2	2.5 L	23×23×5
	12×8×2	3 L	30×20×5
	13×9×2	3.5 L	33×23×5
Loaf Pan	8×4×3	1.5 L	20×10×7
	9×5×3	2 L	23×13×7
Round Layer Cake Pan	8×1½	1.2 L	20×4
	9×1½	1.5 L	23×4
Pie Plate	8×1¼	750 mL	20×3
	9×1¼	1 L	23×3
Baking Dish or Casserole	1 quart	1 L	—
	1½ quart	1.5 L	—
	2 quart	2 L	—